Rex Gunn Was There . . .

At Pearl Harbor on Dec 7th, 1941 . . .

As a member of the radar Signal Corps, Fort Shafter, Oahu, Territory of Hawaii

As a war correspondent during the War in the Pacific . . .

Rex was later appointed correspondent for the 7th Army Corps picture magazine, *BRIEF*, and experienced much of the War in the Pacific from a war correspondent's privileged perspective.

Rex Gunn
Saipan. 1944

As an avid radio "nut", Rex kept current with all the wartime radio programs ... especially those broadcast by the Japanese.

As a radio editor for the Associated Press, assigned to cover the treason trial of Iva Toguri . . .

Rex went to work at the Associated Press in San Francisco in 1949 ... his office just up the street from the courthouse where Iva Toguri was being tried ... and was assigned to cover the trial. He was later able to interview her extensively ... they shared a common involvement in the many events of the War in the Pacific.

As an academic and life-long researcher of the many events encompassed by WWII and the War in the Pacific . . .

After 1949 Rex pursued a lengthy and distinguished academic career during which he was both a teaching professor and administrator at Stanford, UCLA, and U.C. Davis. Throughout this 26-year period Rex continued to research events connected to WWII in the Pacific, and wrote extensively, including this, *They Called Her Tokyo Rose*, *Suddenly ... On A Sunday Morning*, and *Bombs ... For War And Peace*.

"I began writing about WW II in the Pacific as documented fact rather than fiction because I thought that would be simpler. I was wrong. The truth is not only stranger than fiction, it is infinitely more complex."

Rex Gunn

They Called Her

Tokyo Rose

by Rex Gunn

Visit www.booksurge.com for additional copies

First printed in 1977
(2,500 copies for the Japanese-American Citizens League)

Revised 2007
(Re-formatted and edited by Brent Bateman)

Cover artwork © Larry Winkler

ISBN13: 978-0-9796987-0-5

DEDICATION

This book is dedicated to the memory of Iva Ikuko Toguri,
A genuine American patriot and heroine

Iva Toguri passed away in Chicago on September 26th, 2006
She had, it seems, survived them all.

Rex Gunn died at the home of his World War II sweetheart,
Mary Samson Hendrickson
on May 1st, 1999

It was Rex's express wish that all proceeds from this book go to
Mary Hendrickson, who will re-distribute such proceeds to
Iva's surviving family, Rex's former wife and two daughters,
herself, and the editor, as she sees fit.

Brent Bateman, Editor

FOREWORD

Rex Gunn wrote *They Called Her Tokyo Rose* in 1977, the same year that President Gerald Ford gave Iva Toguri a full pardon, restoring her citizenship and righting, at least in part, the grave wrong that had been done to her. He copyrighted his work and self-printed 2,000 copies . . but he never published the book. Copies of the original prints are unavailable, except as they emerge now and then as expensive collector's items.

Rex was there during Iva Toguri's trial in 1949, was finally able to interview her in person following her release from prison in 1956, and he remained in contact with her until his death in 1999. Iva Toguri passed away in September, 2006.

Rex was the first to write a full length account about Iva Toguri and her tragic role as the legendary Tokyo Rose, broadcasting via short wave radio from station JOAK, Radio Tokyo, to the Allied forces fighting in the Pacific arena during World War II. Two notable works have followed, *Tokyo Rose, Orphan of the Pacific*, by Masayo Duus (1979), and *The Hunt For Tokyo Rose*, by Russell W. Howe (1990).

Although Rex had a great story to tell, and could compose wonderfully in a scholarly manner, for he had been a Professor of English Literature at Stanford University . . his writing and formatting style made for strained reading by us more common folk. Before Rex passed away, I made a promise to him that I would re-format and edit his manuscript to make it easier to read, and to get it published. Through his daughter, Sally, Rex gave me the last remaining in-family copy of that original book, and I have published this, a "revised" edition of the same.

The Editor

CHAPTER I

A WILD NIGHT ON OAHU

It was a wild night on Oahu – the night of December 7, 1941. In the aftermath of the stunning Sunday morning attack by Japanese carrier planes on Pearl Harbor, the *Honolulu Advertiser* issued an extra, containing rumors.

Readers were warned to be "on the watch for parachutists reported in Kalihi", for "a party of saboteurs that had been landed on northern Oahu, distinguished by red discs on their shoulders", and for a man of "unannounced nationality" apprehended in the Punch Bowl, "carrying a basket of pigeons" [1]

With the darkness and the rumors had come the first blackout under martial law in Hawaii. Nervous guards triggered machine-gun blasts aimed at wind-blown litter, dogs, cats – anything that moved. GI trucks with their headlights masked by blue cellophane groped their way through unlighted streets.

Few facts were known. Strict censorship was imposed. Among the GIs in Hawaii, Japanese-Americans were presumed to have had something to do with the fantastic success enjoyed by the attacking pilots. There was talk of huge arrows carved in sugar cane fields, pointing the way to Pearl Harbor.

In the wake of the shocking news of the attack on Pearl Harbor, submariners, cruising in U.S. submarines in the waters below the Philippines as far as the South China Seas tuned in on Radio Tokyo. They heard many announcers trumpeting news of the Japanese victory at Pearl Harbor. The cold, hard voice of one woman in particular caught their attention. She was introduced over short wave as "Madame Tojo". Speaking in excellent English, she delivered taunts about the location of the American fleet.

"Where is the United States fleet? I'll tell you where it is, boys. It's lying at the bottom of Pearl Harbor!" [2]

Early on the morning of December 11, 1941, one of those taunts via short wave from Radio Tokyo was picked up by a U.S. submariner, and he recorded it in the ship's log. He wrote:

"Where is the United States fleet?" jeered Tokyo Rose . . . "'I'll tell you where it is, boys. It's lying at the bottom of Pearl Harbor." [3]

As far as anyone has been able to learn from a review of wartime U.S. Navy logs, this was the first time that the name, "**Tokyo Rose**" had been recorded. It was obvious that the recorder had used license in his "quotation" because he had added in the log entry that the announcer had been introduced by a "jujitsu rendition of 'It's Three O'Clock in the Morning ...'" [4]

Clearly, the submariner was allowing his imagination to roam.

Where did he get the name, "**Tokyo Rose**?"

There is no way to be sure. According to Army Air Corps Major Joseph Gervais, the name **Tokyo Rose** was used by construction workers on Saipan in connection with the disappearance of aviatrix Amelia Earhart on a round-the-world flight in 1937. [5]

Gervais said the name was applied to a lanky woman, captive of the Japanese – a woman with red hair and freckles. According to various reports among the workers, Gervais added, the woman call Tokyo Rose had gone to Radio Tokyo as a captive propagandist, or had fallen sick and died, to be buried in an unmarked grave on Saipan, or had been beheaded and buried in a secret grave.

The rumor that a captive Amelia Earhart had become a radio propagandist was persistent. It was officially investigated by the U.S. Army during the war and in the post-war occupation of Japan. [6]

Perhaps the name was linked to Amelia Earhart, but the creation of **Tokyo Rose** need not necessarily have been linked to any actual person. "Roses" abound in American popular song and folklore, i.e., *Rambling Rose, Mexicali Rose, Rose of Washington Square, The Yellow Rose of Texas, Rosie the Riveter, My Wild Irish Rose, Sweet Gypsy Rose*, ad infinitum. It wasn't really necessary that the submariner had to be thinking of any actual broadcaster to come up with a name like **Tokyo Rose**.

Two months later (in February, 1942), the name was linked to a tale about red submarines – a pirate fleet of submarines – in the South China Seas. Once again, the recording was done in a submarine log (the *U.S.S. Seadragon*). When they heard a woman announcer from Radio Tokyo promising "Death to the red submarines!" the crew of the *Seadragon* had a big laugh. The joke, they said, was on **Tokyo Rose**. The *Seadragon* was the only red submarine in the Pacific, and she was red because her black paint had peeled off and she hadn't been able to make port to get another paint job. So, her red-lead undercoat was showing, and when she had entered Soerabaja Straits, *Seadragon* had looked like a boiled lobster. [7]

One month later, **Tokyo Rose** was recorded in the log of another U.S. submarine (*Seawolf*) as the sub cruised off Java, headed for Christmas Island. [8]

By then, **Tokyo Rose** quotations among the growing U.S. forces in the Pacific were legion. One concerned a famous American ace of the war, Navy Lt. Edward H. (Butch) O'Hare, who had shot down five Japanese planes on February 20, 1942. After Butch O'Hare was given a hero's welcome back in the States, *Yank Magazine* quoted **Tokyo Rose**, and in the quotation something new was added (another nickname) linking the Pacific siren to the infamous English traitor at Radio Berlin – Lord Haw Haw:

> *"The Japs jeered. Butch O'Hare was a one-battle fighter, they said. He was afraid to return to the Pacific. Tokyo Rose, Japan's Lady Haw Haw, declared he was probably dead."* [9]

As of April, 1942, American fortunes in the Pacific war were at low ebb. The Philippines, Guam, Wake Island, the Solomon Islands, New Britain, Malaya, and Java had fallen to the Japanese. Captive allied forces by the thousands were being shuffled through Pacific ports by the Japanese. Many died. All were uncertain whether they would ever be free again. The last American resistance in the Philippines was being worn down at Bataan and Corregidor. Those were grim days for Americans in the Pacific.

Recalling those days, a correspondent who was saved from capture on Bataan by a last-minute rescue via submarine (Associated Press's Clark Lee) wrote:

> *"The story that Radio Tokyo invariably knew every move made by the American Army is one of the most persistent of the war. It began shortly after Pearl Harbor, and as far back as April, 1942, when a group of us escaped from Bataan and reached Australia, we were told that Radio Tokyo had reported our arrival and had said, 'Glad you made it to Australia. We'll be down after you before long.'*

> *"When a fight squadron or a bomber group moved to a new base, dozens of people reported that Tokyo Rose had said, 'Hello, there, you boys of the Three Hundred and Nineteenth. Hope you'll enjoy the Philippines more than you did New Guinea."*

"Every new transfer was supposed to be announced by Tokyo *the day that it was made. However, I never found anyone who actually had heard such broadcasts himself. It was always the guy in the next tent." [10]*

Lee, eventually, would be the man who would file a sensational post-war story on "the one and only **Tokyo Rose**" as an American traitor.

So, Bataan fell. Corregidor fell. To be an American GI stationed at one of the endangered outposts west of Hawaii was to live in constant fear. From our pre-war state of confidence, in which we had pictured ourselves protected by "invincible Pearl Harbor", [11] we had been alarmed by one defeat after another, stretching almost 3,000 miles from the Philippines to Midway. Now, each one of us knew, the next large land mass to fall to the Japanese (unless the crippled U.S. Navy could stop them in mid-ocean), would be the Hawaiian Islands.

During that time I was serving as a member of the Signal Corps (the author). Daily, we watched the skies for reassuring swarms of American war planes. Surely, we thought, we would be reinforced so that we could gain air supremacy over the Japanese. But we watched in vain. No swarms of planes were sent – not even a trickle. American air power was being directed to the European Theatre. It occurred to each of us that we, too, might be sacrificed to the higher priority for American arms in the European Theatre.

By the end of May, 1942, **Tokyo Rose** "quotes" were credited with virtually every rumor about American troop movements in the Pacific. The legend winged far ahead of any actual propaganda from Radio Tokyo. For example, the vision of **Tokyo Rose** had expanded to include the formidable authority of "The Dragon Lady" – Tojo's girl Friday According to the GIs, the whole shooting match was being broadcasted by **Tokyo Rose**. She knew everything – knew which outfit was moving to which island – knew when and why. And as likely as not she would call the C.O. by name and rank. When she promised a plane's hot reception, they got one; and when she forecasted bombings, we got bombed.

That was the original, authentic, GI **Tokyo Rose** – a news caster, not a disc jockey or a torch singer, or a nostalgia peddler as she was later pictured to be. Prior to the Battle of Midway (June 4 - 6, 1942), there was nothing playful about her. We credited her voice as the voice of our daily fears. Her roll call of our outfits on the move sounded like the crack of doom. We figured that all of us had about as much chance to get back home alive as the men of Torpedo Squadron Eight had to get back to the *Hornet* (during the famous bombing raid on Tokyo on April 18th, 1942, it was necessary to launch the B-25 bombers 500 miles further from their target than planned, with the knowledge that they would not have enough fuel to be able to return to the carrier *Hornet)*. **Tokyo Rose** was not a joke. The laughter she caused was grim and bitter. She was the victorious enemy.

Even after the U.S. Navy turned back the Japanese fleet at Midway, **Tokyo Rose** continued to be the unofficial greeter at virtually every island occupied by the Allied forces, and her messages continued to be grim.

"Hey, you GI's on Guadalcanal! . . . Your island is mined with TNT. Anyone still there after 24 hours will be blown sky high." [12]

"Greetings to the bloody butchers of Guadalcanal. Welcome to Cape Gloucester. We've been expecting you." [13]

"This program is dedicated to the Jolly Rogers, the 90th Bomb Group. I know you are moving from Dobodura to Nadzab, New Guinea, on January 17th, and I will have a reception committee there waiting for you." [14]

"Congratulations, Commander Perry, on your safe landing (on Abemama in the Gilberts). *But you will be sorry if you don't leave soon or now."* [15]

But the victories in the new battles were becoming ours now. At last, we were on the winning side. Hundreds of thousands of fresh American troops and swarms of friendly planes were arriving in the Pacific. With them came a fresh image of **Tokyo Rose.** The GI attitude toward her became increasingly playful.

When seabees were building an airfield on Saipan in the summer of 1944, so the story went, **Tokyo Rose** came on the air and said, "Confidentially, boys, your strip is showing."

When a general's house caught fire in the Aleutians while the general was en route to the states in a plane, **Tokyo Rose** beamed a special message to the general's radio operator, telling the crew to return to the Aleutians so that the general could save his home.

Another Aleutian story attributed to **Rose** was a thank-you broadcast for the use of an air base photo lab, entered one night by members of a Japanese submarine crew who sneaked ashore to develop some pictures of geisha girls.

Still another of **Tokyo Rose's** stories, current in the Seventh Army Air Corps circles, told of an admiral's special swimming pool on Lady Slipper Island off Kwajalein, built from war materials by seabees and "staffed" by U.S. Army and Navy nurses. On moonlit nights, so the tale went, crews returning from bombing missions could see the nude nurses swimming about in the admiral's pool.

Meanwhile, by the spring of 1944, Roses by many other names had sprung up before microphones not only at Radio Tokyo, but at Manila, in Indonesia, Java, and at Shanghai. None was introduced as **Tokyo Rose**. But among the GIs at the receiving end, all were called **Tokyo Rose.**

During this later period, a New York Times article described the new **Tokyo Rose** as an entertainer and spread her fame to millions of new readers. The headline read:

'TOKYO ROSE' A HIT

WITH U.S. SOLDIERS'

"If a radio popularity poll could be taken out here among American fighting forces a surprisingly large number of votes would go to 'Tokyo Rose' and others of the programs beamed from the Land of the Rising Sun".

"Tokyo programs might even be voted first place '"

"Tokyo is entertaining. Tokyo gives the listener's comedy and good dance music ... The men say they get the most music from the five Tokyo programs they hear regularly." [16]

Obviously, **Tokyo Rose** was getting a new image. But the *New York Times* article had raised more questions than it had answered about that image. It had not named "the five programs heard regularly" [17] from Radio Tokyo, and had not even mentioned the red-hot mama of Japanese radio – the low-moaning, torch singing woman sometimes called "Myrtle" and at other times "Margie" at the Japanese station, Radio Manila.

She came on with "Auld Lang Syne" by Guy Lombardo and went off with an equally nostalgic version of "Aloha", sandwiching in between pitiful condolences for all of "you boys" who were dying out there in the muck and jungle while their wives and sweethearts at home were out with the 4-F's and defenses workers, spending the big money.

Finally, the U.S. Army decided to find out what was actually being broadcast to Allied forces by Japanese sirens in the Pacific. To do that job, the Office of War Information sent a Hollywood movie writer, Lieutenant Colonel Ted E. Sherdeman, head of Armed Forces Radio, to Australia late in 1943.

Sherdeman had another mission as well. Once he had analyzed who or what was meant by **Tokyo Rose**, and what she was doing that was so popular among GI's in the Pacific, he meant to lure away her audience, using GI talent.

Sherdeman quickly identified the old **Tokyo Rose** legend as centering on "Madame Tojo" of Radio Tokyo, and the sexy, tantalizing voice of Margie at Radio Manila – and the new playmate legend as focused on a woman, a newcomer, with a staccato voice like a WAC drill sergeant, who called herself "Orphan Ann" on the previously all-male "Zero Hour".

The "Zero Hour" was beamed on the 19 and 25-meter bands at 6:00 p.m. (Tokyo Time) to catch GI's as they lined up for chow in the Central and South Pacific.

It opened with "Strike Up The Band" and closed with a peppy version of "Goodbye Now". The music stayed peppy with a lot of marches and semi-classical stuff by the Boston Pops Orchestra.

To lure away Orphan Ann's audience Sherdeman created the "Sarong Network" or "Mosquito Network", using GI disc jockeys such as "Boondock Barney" and "Gizmo" on Armed Forces stations at Eniwetok, Kwajalein, Saipan, Guam, and other locations.

But shipping space aboard transport planes and ships was scarce, and the GI disc jockeys were hard put to get late recordings from the States. So, their music libraries were no more up to date than Radio Tokyo's. In spite of the Armed Forces Radio efforts, the legendary **Tokyo Rose** continued to lead the hit parade in the Pacific, with "Madame Tojo" leading the pack of actual broadcasters as news announcer and "Orphan Ann" of "Zero Hour" in the spotlight as disc jockey, with Radio Manila's Margie mysteriously intervening with her sexy voice and haunting mockery. .

Meanwhile, at the same time that **Tokyo Rose** had made the big time in the *New York Times*, news of the Pacific siren filtered into Radio Tokyo via a Swedish magazine story, reprinted from the New York articles. Prior to April, 1944, the actual broadcasters at Radio Tokyo had never heard of the name **Tokyo Rose.** Now they looked about among themselves with excited surmise. Somebody among them apparently had become famous. Who was she?

CHAPTER II

ORPHAN ANN OF "ZERO HOUR"

So the woman known as "Orphan Ann of "Zero Hour" was almost as much a mystery at Radio Tokyo as she was to her GI listeners in the South Pacific. From the time that she had started broadcasting in November of '43, she spent only about thirty minutes at the radio station each day, arriving at ten of six, then leaving immediately after her broadcast at 6:15 or 6:20. She wasted no time getting out of there. Except for the tall, mustached leader of the Allied war prisoners, Australian Major Charles (Bill) Cousens, she had no friends, no confident, and no acquaintance with whom she exchanged more than a few words at Radio Tokyo.

The Japanese who knew most about her were members of the military secret police, the Kempei tai. And the one policeman who knew her best was Master Sergeant Katsuo Okada of the Thought Control Section, who was charged to keep her under surveillance.

From his surveillance, Okada had come to know a great deal about her. Each weekend, she disguised herself – changing from the appearance as a mature young woman in her late twenties to a teenager who went foraging for food. As food had become scarce in Tokyo in late 1943, many families sent their younger members foraging through the countryside, so it attracted no undue attention when a skinny girl with braided hair spent her weekends bartering scarce goods for food. She was typical, that is, except that she wore blue jeans and American oxfords, and could speak only limited Japanese.

She was slight of build, appearing to be somewhere between 16 and 19 years old, and she had a mole above her lip. She carried with her woolen clothing, soap, sugar, and salt (all were scarce commodities in the countryside, and even hard to find in the stores of Tokyo), which she traded for vegetables and fruits. Early Saturday morning, she would begin her journey, walking 10 to 15 miles, seldom revisiting any one home. On Sunday nights she might be seen lugging pumpkins or potatoes or onions; tangerines, apples, lemons, pears; or eggs, flour, rice, bread, and oatmeal back to the city.

From the looks of her, she ate very little herself, for her arms and legs seemed ready to snap from the weight of a large pumpkin or a sack of potatoes.

On weekdays, one could hardly recognize her as the same person. Wearing her hair waved, dressed in oxfords and a suit, she would leave her room in Setagaya-ku and walk to the Danish legation compound in Kojimachi-ku. There she would enter an old house which appeared from the outside to be of solid masonry, but from the inside it became clear that the structure was of wood, with only a masonry exterior. This was the headquarters of Danish Minister Lars Tillitse.

The woman's path then led up the stately wooden staircase into the reception rooms where the floors were inlaid with beautiful designs and the ceilings and panels were of maple and cherry wood. Here she served from 8:30 a.m. to 4:30 or 5:00 p.m. each weekday as receptionist and personal secretary to the Minister.

When she left the Danish legation, she would take a bus downtown, getting off in front of Radio Tokyo. After half an hour or 45 minutes, she returned to the street, usually with a young man who did not appear to be Japanese.

In the evenings, she sometimes could be found standing in line for hours at some Tokyo tobacconist or making the rounds of the city's drug stores and pharmacies, searching for quantities of vitamin tablets, yeast tablets, quinine, whale oil, and aspirin. As if her needs were insatiable, she also dealt on the black market with cash for the same goods: food, drugs, tobacco.

All that she collected seemed to vanish as quickly as she got it, and she remained as thin as ever. From December, 1943, to August, 1945, her average weekly forage supply would have kept alive a large family in Japan, yet this woman had to be treated for malnutrition, pellagra, and beri beri.

In the neighborhood where she lived, which was called Onarikin House at 396 Ike Jiri Street, Setagaya-ku, it was well known that the military police and the Tokyo police each had two agents watching the woman, for the officers had talked not only to the young lady's landlady, Mrs. Unami Kido, but to the neighbor women as well, and they referred to the girl, who had come to Japan just before the war as a visitor from America, as "horyo", which is a loose way of saying "war prisoner" or "traitor", directly implying that she was an enemy.

The young woman, as all the neighbors knew, bought no war bonds, gave no clothing or old jewels or old metals to the neighborhood organization for helping the war effort, refused to change her citizenship from American to Japanese, and could be heard speaking English, mostly to the small man who was often seen with her – a Domei News Agency wire newsman named Felipe (Phil) d'Aquino. He also, it was known, was a foreigner, a Portuguese, whose father had been interned as a dangerous enemy alien in the mountain resort town of Karuizawa.

Master Sergeant Katsuo Okada had ready access to all of this talk among the neighbors, since he was the nephew of Mr. and Mrs. Kido – Mr. Kido was in the Japanese Army in Manchuria – and was a frequent visitor in his aunt's boarding house. Mrs. Kido had sought his advice before allowing the American woman to move in.

"You will have trouble", he told his aunt, "because she is known as pro-American, but if you caution her to be careful and you, yourself, are careful, it will be all right".

Mrs. Kido's brother-in-law, who lived next door to her, became so angry that he refused to speak with Mrs. Kido afterwards, but Mrs. Kido liked the American girl and would not make her move.

That was alright with Sgt. Okada, for it made his investigations of the girl a simple matter. Plus, the neighbors didn't even have to be asked; they rushed forward with their various tales.

"This girl was seen on the bus", one told Okada, "as it passed the emperor's palace she refused to bow, and when another passenger told her to bow, she got off the bus at the next corner".

It was a neighbor who found out about the Christmas tree, too. Mrs. Kido wouldn't have said anything, but the neighbor saw the American girl taking the small fir tree into her house, and she saw through the window the girl trimming the tree with popcorn strings and other such baubles. She realized that it was an American ceremony, and she spread the news all through the neighborhood, causing Mrs. Kido to warn the girl that she had better take the Christmas tree down. It was against the law to have one. The girl had refused, but her Portuguese friend finally took it away.

Sgt. Okada knew three things about the young American woman for which he could have arrested her at any time. For one, he knew that she was disposing of her food and medicine supplies at Radio Tokyo. When the girl entered Radio Tokyo each evening shortly before six o'clock, she had with her a shopping bag with supplies in it. But when she emerged from the building some 30 or 40 minutes later, her shopping bag was empty.

Since she worked with the war prisoners, Okada notified the Kampei tai man who watched the prisoners, Officer Sawada. Sawada later noted that the prisoners often carried food back to the camp in their clothing, after leaving Radio Tokyo, where they worked.

Strangely, although Sawada had reported this, nothing was done to prevent the girl from continuing to gather food and pass it on to the war prisoners. Okada himself was glad that no action was taken, for he had seen the war prisoners who were forced to broadcast under the radio boss, Tsuneishi, and he would estimate that they averaged about 40 pounds underweight.

The second thing for which Okada could arrest the woman, Toguri, at any time was for her habit of saying that Japan would lose the war. He felt that if she thought that America would win the war, then she should at least keep it to herself, but she had said it even to Okada, and he had warned her, taking great pains to let her know how dangerous it was.

"You, as a person who had long residence in the United States, you may think you know the strength of the United States. You may truly think that it is correct when you say America is going to win the war. But I don't want to think such a thing, and neither does anyone else. For you to talk about that is violating Japanese law, and I caution you that you better not talk about this to others. If you talk about such things to people other than myself, you will be investigated by the Kempei gendarmes and the Metropolitan Police. I am a Kempei, but I am also your friend. I don't want to accuse you of the crime, but I am going to caution you of this as a friend."

Okada also tried to tell Iva about the forced internment of Japanese-Americans living in states such as her beloved California by the U.S. government. Iva adamantly refused to believe such a thing had happened.

Sgt. Okada knew one other thing about the young American woman, Toguri. During the whole time that she aided the prisoners with food, tobacco, and drugs, she and her Portuguese friend, d'Aquino, had also been typing copies of war news received through Domei listening posts from American sources.

These Allied news items she had taken to Radio Tokyo and slipped to the prisoners of war: which was, of course, a violation of orders because war prisoners were to receive no war news from any foreign sources.

But Okada, again, did not arrest her because he was interested in those foreign items of news himself, and it did seem that Japan was losing the war.

Okada considered the woman no less a war prisoner than the men with whom she broadcast on the "Zero Hour". He felt no fear that she would extend her resistance to the war effort past the point of aid to the prisoners.

This was because even the Japanese employees at Radio Tokyo did not discuss their work openly with other employees, and especially not with outsiders. One never knew when he or she might be talking to a plain clothes member of the Kempeis and say the wrong thing. It was best to say little and confide in no one.

So, when the Swedish article about Tokyo Rose arrived at Radio Tokyo in April, 1944, there was no open meeting about it – no official effort to determine who was meant by it. But there was talk – mostly in whispers – that it could be Ruth Hayakawa, an announcer with a soft voice and Boston accent. Or Fumi Saisho, the hard-voiced "Madame Tojo". Or Iva Toguri, in her role as "Orphan Ann". Or it could have been any one of several others.

But nothing official was done about it, and the two ex-American Nisei supervisors of "Zero Hour" – George Nakamoto, formerly of San Francisco, and Ken Oki, who had grown up in Sacramento – did not change anyone's broadcast name to fit the news. However, it did occur to them that, at some future time, someone could profit by the name – or suffer because of it, if the Americans should win the war.

CHAPTER III

HOW THE NIGHTMARE BEGAN

The bombing of Pearl Harbor on December 7th, 1941, and the announcement of war the next day had hit Japanese homes with every bit as much surprise as it did American ones. Iva's uncle told her about the bombing and the declaration of war – Iva couldn't understand the radio broadcasts nor read the papers. When told, she simply couldn't believe that such a thing had happened.

On December 8th, two police agents from Setagaya Ward came to see her at her uncle's house. They told her that Mr. Fujiwara of the Japanese special police was interested to know what she was going to do.

"It would be a good idea for you to take out Japanese citizenship," one of them had suggested.

To become a Japanese citizen was quite simple for the more than 10,000 Nisei, caught by the war in Japan. They could do it by registering in the "koseki", their Japanese family registers which were maintained as public records. Iva had been registered in her family koseki by relatives, at the request of her father, when she was two months and several days old on Sept. 13, 1916. Her name had been scratched out of the koseki, again at her father's request, when she was sixteen, on Jan 13, 1932, when it became illegal under American law to hold both Japanese and United States citizenship.

Iva was informed that she had only to have her name written in again to gain full privileges as a Japanese citizen. That would mean no more trips to the police station as an alien, no wrangling for travel visas and special ration cards, peace with her relatives, and less suspicion from their neighbors. Many American Nisei caught in Japan by the war were doing that – in fact, nearly all of them were taking out Japanese citizenship. Iva, however, stubbornly resolved that she never would.

The *Tatsuta Maru* had turned back to Japan in mid-passage, so nothing had been lost by Iva's failure to gain passage on that ship. Her next chance had come in February, two months after the start of the war. She had seen a note in an English-language newspaper, the daily Mainichi, saying that the Swiss legation in Tokyo was accepting applications for American evacuees to the United States. The ship was the *U.S.S. Gripsholm*. Iva applied immediately. Her application got as far as the second secretary of the Swiss legation, Mr. Micheli, who informed her that her American citizenship was in doubt – that the status of all Japanese-Americans, even those in the United States, was in doubt. So Ambassador Drew and his party of several hundred other Americans, but not Iva, sailed on the *Grissholm*. She thus suffered her second incident of discrimination – this time at the hands of the Americans.

Iva was spending her passage money to live on by then, and the pressure either to become a Japanese citizen or move out of her aunt and uncle's home was becoming more intense.

"She is *horyo* – an enemy", more than one of his neighbors said to him.

"No, no", Hajemi Hattori said, "she is not an enemy. She is just a woman. Pay no attention to what she says."

"Then why is she here?"

"She came to visit because her mother is sick."

"Her mother is sick? Then let her go back to her sick mother1"

There really was no explaining it to them. Police agents of the Kompei tai had been coming to Hajemi Hattori's house regularly, and the neighbors were becoming frightened, which made them even angrier at Hajemi. The worst of it was that she did say foolish things. She said openly in Hajemi's house that the Japanese had started the war, that the Americans would win, and she hoped it would be quickly. It was all too much. She knew that she had to move.

She had begun searching for work as soon as she had been denied passage on the *Gripsholm* in February, but she couldn't get work because she was a U.S. citizen. It was too risky for the Japanese to employ her, even if she could do the work, and there was little work she could do in Japan. She couldn't read Japanese. She had only a very shaky knowledge of conversational Japanese. She couldn't do any interpreting. She couldn't translate.

Matsuniya, the Japanese language school principal, let her earn her tuition at the school by typing an English translation of a grammar book he had written, and by giving piano lessons to his children at 5 yen per lesson (less 21/2 yen for rental of the piano), but this did nothing to offset her living expenses. It couldn't even be counted on to offset the school tuition. She earned a total of 20 yen per month with the piano lessons and the tuition was 30 yen per month. She quit the language school in late spring.

By this time she was well into her cash reserves – the $300 for passage back to the United States. She walked the streets for three months and searched each English-language newspaper she could lay her hands on until she finally saw an ad for an English-language typist. She applied and got the job as a part-time typist-monitor at the Ataga Hill listening outpost of the Domei News Agency in Tokyo. Her job was to monitor American and Allied News via shortwave for five hours a day, five days a week at a salary of 110 yen per month (less a 25 per cent tax deduction). That left just enough to cover her room and board at her new residence – Onarikin House in Shiba Ward, Tokyo (65 yen a month for room and two meals per day).

At the time that she had moved from her uncle's place, in June, she learned that her family in California was incarcerated in the Gila River Relocation Camp, in Arizona. She tried to write them, but nothing was ever returned. She of course had hopes of being able to pay her way back to the United States if she could get in touch with her father. Jun Toguri had been very successful in his Los Angeles grocery and import business, but it was impossible to know what his financial condition might be now that he was in a relocation camp. Iva wondered about that term, "relocation camp". What exactly did that mean?

She had talked about her situation with her acquaintances, Chiyeko Ito and Yoniko Matsunaga, in visits to the Waseda International Institute in Tokyo where they were attending school. They were also American Nisei.

"Can they make you become a Japanese citizen?" was the question uppermost in each of their minds.

"They can never make you take out Japanese citizenship because that is your prerogative", said Iva.

"They can intern you", one answered.

"Yes, they can, but no one can make you become a Japanese citizen."

The job at Domei's Ataga Hill outpost had done two important things for Iva: it put her in contact with news of the war which she could understand and interpret. She received news reports via short wave from Hawaii, San Francisco, New York, and London. She heard the commentaries of William Winter and H.V. Kaltenborn. Then, the Domei job also put her in contact with a man whom she liked very much and in whom she felt she could confide. He was Felipe (Phil) d'Aquino, three quarters Japanese in his parentage but a Portuguese citizen. The two of them agreed that Japan wasn't doing as well as was claimed in the Japanese domestic news releases. Occasionally Iva had the opportunity to buy an English-language newspaper printed in Japan, but the news it gave was the opposite of what she heard from San Francisco and London via shortwave radio.

D'Aquino also had helped her to secure food – she hadn't been able to get a ration card from June to about September of 1942, because of police pressure. She was being visited in her new residency by three separate types of police – police from the Kempei tai; police from the metropolitan office in Tokyo, and police from Shiba prefecture. All three had their "tokko tai" (thought control) divisions and that was what they applied to Iva's case. Foreigners were under the jurisdiction of the tokko tai divisions. She had to have a police permit for a ration card, for travel outside of Tokyo, and a renewal of her visitor's permit every six months (ironically, in order to be able to stay in Japan). In their periodic visits, the police agents always brought up the advisability of securing Japanese citizenship.

In September of 1942 the Swiss legation announced that Americans might be repatriated on a second ship which would go from Yokohama to Gura, India, and from there to New York. Passengers would need $425 in cash either before they boarded ship or before they disembarked at New York. But Iva had exhausted her cash which was to have paid her return passage, which had been only $300 in the beginning, anyway. By then she had no money at all, and she could not contact her family. She couldn't pay for the passage and she had no prospect of being able to pay. Her take home pay from Domei amounted to less than $5.00 per month in American money. She was forced to cancel her application with the Swiss Legation for passage.

There remained the hope that the war would be over soon. The Domei listening outpost was one of the few places in Japan where one had an opportunity to hear American interpretations of the Pacific War. Iva noted that William Winter, in particular, referenced all in his communiqués about Allied advances in the Pacific to the Battles of Midway and the Coral Sea.

CHAPTER IV

MIDWAY . . . THE TIDE BEGINS TO TURN

"This was the turning point", he said repeatedly, and Iva thought that he was right. She said as much in conversations with other workers at Domei, namely three men named Nagamoto, Sawato, and Nakano, in addition to her friend, Felipe d'Aquino, and a girl named Sumiyashi.

Nagamoto in particular scoffed at the Allied reports of Naval victories and said they couldn't believe anything the Americans said.

Iva retorted, "How do you account for it . . . that since the Battle of Midway and the Battle of the Coral Sea the Japanese never name any ships that they claim to have sunk, never name any aircraft carriers . . . but the Americans always bring out the exact name of the Japanese ships and aircraft carriers and anytime they do you never hear of that ship again?"

Nagamoto flushed. "Maybe you think the Americans are winning because you want them to win."

"I am saying that we are getting the truth from the Allied news sources and not from the Japanese reports."

"Maybe somebody should tell the Kempei tai that you know more about the war than they do."

D'Aquino became angered at Nagamoto's threat to report Iva and the argument, which went on sporadically for several weeks, ended in a fist fight between Nagamoto and d'Aquino. Iva knew that Nagamoto had been bluffing. He wouldn't go near the police of his own accord. Everybody at Domei, even the Japanese nationals, wanted as little attention from the police as possible. Perhaps Nagamoto would not report her, but he succeeded in convincing the others that her views were a danger to them all.

The police didn't really alarm her until February, 1943. She had received added pressure after cancelling her application for ship's passage at the Swiss legation. They came immediately after for an interview with her. Her landlady, Mrs. Furuya, and Mrs. Furura's teenage daughter were there. There were three agents this time. Mrs. Furuya interpreted their questions.

"What reason is there now to keep you from becoming a Japanese citizen?" one of them asked her.

"The same reasons", she said.

These same three became regular visitors. They never stayed for long. The manner of the visits seemed casual. But then in February came a more alarming type of visit and a direct warning.

Iva came home from work to find the same three agents there, and her room turned inside out. They had searched through her books, her trunk, her papers, and they had made no effort to rearrange things. The books were left open. This time they were in plain clothes – she was alone with them and she was thoroughly frightened.

She said, "Why are you doing this?"

"Oh . . . we are looking for things written in English."

"Things about Japan government in English. We better not find anything against Japan government here – or you be sorry."

They left and Iva tried to reconstruct the purpose behind this latest visit. Perhaps someone had told them that she was saying pro-American things at Domei. Nagamoto or one of the others could have done in anonymously. She decided then that she had better leave Domei, for things wouldn't get any better. The feelings against her would only become worse as Japan's losses became more obvious. She discussed this with Felipe and he agreed that it probably would be a good idea, but that she should hold on until she found another job, which wouldn't be easy.

She had been looking for another job all along because her income wasn't enough to live on, but now she really began to work at it. She visited all the foreign legations and hope was held out to her by the Danish Consul, Lars Tillitse, but the opening would not occur for maybe a year.

By the summer of 1943 her situation had become desperate again. She simply had not been making enough money to live on and was under constant emotional pressures at Domei. She finally contracted beri beri and had to be hospitalized for about six weeks, beginning in June of '43. Her doctor, K. Amano, warned her to eat more fresh fruits and vegetables.

Every facet of normal living had taken on a nightmarish complexity. For example, there was the business of finding a newspaper she could read. She didn't have enough money to subscribe to one so it became a major diplomatic enterprise with her to find copies of English language newspapers. Asking for them usually aroused suspicion. She occasionally skipped a meal so that she could buy the English-language Nippon Times, but she couldn't do this often.

She looked so completely Japanese that local people could never understand that the language was difficult for her. By this time, she may have added some sort of emotional block to her comprehension of the language. At any rate, she was a very poor student of Japanese.

The ad for the job which finally appeared in the Nippon Times didn't look like much at all, but it was the first English language opening which had appeared for months. It read: "A few jobs for typists in the English language open at Radio Tokyo."

She was required to take a competitive examination and wait several days for the results. Then she was notified that she had the job. She was to begin work August 23, 1943, in the third floor business office under Mr. Sheigecheka Takano. She was to work only for two or three hours per day, six days a week. But if she could hold on to the Domei job for a while longer, she could double her income, because the Radio Tokyo job paid 100 yen per month (less the usual 25% tax). That would be enough money for doctor bills and food again.

Radio Tokyo was a large operation in one of the most modern buildings in Japan. There was a long row of typists doing highly impersonal work. Iva felt that she could lose herself in this office for the duration, and perhaps stay out of trouble—that is, if she could avoid conversations about who started the war, who was winning it, and so on.

That resolve was overthrown on her second day at Radio Tokyo, on the afternoon of August 24, 1943, while she was talking to one of the staff announcers, Ruth Hayakawa. Three emaciated white men had entered the overseas section which adjoined the business office. They looked like scarecrows. Two guards accompanied them.

Iva' heart had gone out to them. It had been so long since Iva had seen any Americans except Nisei – any group who felt and thought as she did. She hadn't questioned for a moment what she would do. She would take the first pretext she could find to talk to them, to introduce herself.

That's how it had all begun – the connection between Iva and Tokyo Rose.

CHAPTER V

AID AND COMFORT TO THE POWs

At Radio Tokyo, Iva Toguri found that she could take the short walk from the third floor business office to the second floor PW (Prisoners of War) room at Radio Tokyo without attracting undue attention, so long as she carried mimeographed and typewritten materials and displayed a calm show of business decorum. Dozens of people bustled constantly about the halls, including couriers from Domei, visitors and guests, as well as employees.

Through the last week in August and all of September, 1943, Iva visited the PW room almost daily. The two guards, one of whom stood just outside the PW room at all times, apparently didn't speak English. They accepted her presence as routine. However, the very ease with which she was able to come and go increased suspicion of her among the prisoners.

During the first weeks each limited his conversation with her to a brief greeting and a casual "thank you" whenever she slipped them Allied news dispatches from Domei, which she frequently did. She asked no questions of them. Instead, she talked about herself. She talked to them about her student days at UCLA – about her favorite spectator sport, football, of her unlucky trip to Japan, her inability to get out, her dislike of militarists, and her repeated refusals to accept Japanese citizenship.

Guardedly, they asked her for medicine, food and tobacco. She immediately began to make daily deliveries of quinine, aspirin, lemons, and a variety of foods. She hid them in her purse, her clothing, or among papers, and passed them along in the PW room.

The American captain, Wallace Ince, began to kid her about the "Hollywood Branch" of the University of California (he had attended the university's home campus at Berkeley). Reyes began to talk about the Philippines.

During these early conversations, Iva could feel the silent Cousens watching and listening intently. An Australian, he shared no homeland background with her as Ince did. It was natural that he should not take part in the banter about UCLA – but Iva could sense him probing for her motives – listening for some false sound, some hint of deception.

She knew from the way that Ince and Reyes automatically deferred to Cousens that he ultimately would make the decision of whether or not she could be trusted, and accepted.

She recognized the first purposeful talk he started with her sometime in mid-October. It was in the small PW room, which adjoined the record library. Ince was busy. The guard was just outside the door. Cousens glanced up from an Allied news dispatch which she had given him.

"You know, Radio Tokyo is full of kempeis – even the Japanese have to be careful."

"I've been watched by the Kempeis ever since the war started", Iva answered matter-of-factly. She told about the weekly visits of police agents to her uncle's home, her forced move, and about finding her room ransacked at Mrs. Furuya's rooming house. Cousens nodded.

"They have one watching us at the "hotel" (The Dai Ichi Hotel, where the PWs broadcasting at Radio Tokyo were quartered). Here as well – we don't know who it is here."

He told her about being confronted over a conversation on Allied progress in the war which he had with a Dutchman in the Dai Ichi Hotel.

"The room had been wired", he said ruefully. "And the Dutchman had admitted the conversation to them before I denied it."

Iva talked less about herself in the days that followed that first conversation, and silently encouraged Cousens' confidence.

Cousens told Iva that the men at Bunka Prison Camp (in Tokyo) were being starved and beaten and tortured, that they were forced to broadcast contrary to international law under threat of death. He painted a vivid description of the water-torture death of a Chinese coolie (forced to drink continuously from a water hose until he drowned) and the fatal beating of an Australian soldier on the docks at Singapore.

On another day, he told her about Major Tsuneishi, the Army boss of Radio Tokyo, and what had happened when Cousens had protested in writing about being forced to broadcast.

"I was taken into his office", Cousens recalled, "and I told him that I couldn't broadcast anything except messages to prisoners of war and appeals to the Red Cross. I was told to stand in front of him. He was standing at a table with his sword on the table, ready to put to use. Then Tsuneishi read an order in Japanese, which was translated into English to me. The substance was that, if I ever refused another order by any Japanese at Radio Tokyo, I would be executed.

"Tsuneishi is one of the most powerful men in Japan", Cousens told her. "He requests anything he wants under the letterhead of Sombo Hombu (Imperial Japanese Headquarters in Tokyo), and not even generals can deny such requests."

It was in response to a "request" from Tsuneishi, Cousens told Iva, that generals in the field had sent Cousens from Singapore, Ince from Corregidor (where he had handled the "Voice of Freedom" broadcasts under U.S.A General Wainwright), and Reyes from Manila.

"With Tsuneishi, you do just what you are told", Cousens warned her. "Eventually you do just what you are told or you die."

The only weapons which the PWs had against Tsuneishi were their long experience in radio broadcasting (Cousens and Ince between then had 20 years of radio production), and the relative inexperience and lack of talent in the Nisei supervisors, Nakamoto and Oki.

Tsuneishi paid no attention to operational details. He left that to his subordinates.

When Nakamoto and Oki defaulted on script writing or shirked supervisory work, Cousens fashioned the program to his own purposes. He used Japanese character cliches familiar to Americans and Australians. He programmed Gilbert and Sullivan – even The Mikado, which was banned from Japanese broadcasting stations. He repeated key propaganda words until they fell on the ear with ludicrous effect. He spoke cheerfully where a solemn tone would have served the scripted Japanese purpose. He put incongruous subject matter into rapid succession. He read news and commentaries (the chief vehicles of propaganda) too fast or too slowly – too brightly or too solemnly. He deliberately committed an infinite number of technical errors in announcing, programming, and directing.

Ince added to the damage by reading news as fast as 200 words per minute so that it was unintelligible, by scraping needles across records during his shift on the turntables and by leaving microphone switches open so that incongruous studio noises distorted the program. They ran the gamut of operational errors in so far as they dared.

"We've got this operation going just about the way we want it", Cousens told Iva shortly after the first of November. "As propaganda, it's a laugh."

Only a few days later the pudgy Nakamoto entered the PW room with an imperial Japanese order, a final manifest of a Tsuneishi "suggestion" to the Overseas Broadcasting Committee. It had come down the six echelons from the committee to the National Broadcasting Corporation of Japan, to Radio Tokyo, to Mr. Muto (the pre-war Japanese Consul at San Francisco), to Mssrs. Sawada and Takano, and finally to Nakamoto.

Nakamoto fished out of his pocket a rough outline of his ideas for the expansion. Reyes wasn't present at the time. Ince took one look at the crumpled paper and said, "the hell with it."

"Look", said Nakamoto plaintively, "this is an Imperial Order. It has got to be done. It is my neck as well as yours." He did a little chopping business at the neck – a gesture which he often used to persuade prisoners that they had no choice.

Cousens came to look at what Nakamoto had outlined, stared at it, and looked at Nakamoto with disgust.

"Its supposed to be a 'homesicky' program", said Nakamoto.

"All right", said Cousens. "Get out of here and we'll se what we can do. But it won't be like this."

Nakamoto left and Ince turned on Cousens: "What the hell do you mean, 'we'? I want no part of this."

"Hold your horses . . . hold your horses," said Cousens and he began to scribble something on a sheet of paper. "I think this is our chance to make a complete shambles of the Zero Hour."

"How?" asked Ince suspiciously.

"We'll use a woman," cousens continued to write.

"Who?"

"The only one we can trust – Iva Toguri."

Ince shook his head, "You're crazy."

Then he thought about it and he began to laugh.

"Do you think we can get away with it?"

They talked it over. Cousens finished his writing, then went to Nakamoto with the new format.

Plenty of experienced female announcers were available at Radio Tokyo for the type of "homesicky program" which Tsuneishi had suggested.

June Suyama was easily the most exciting female personality – with good vocal range and control who got choice announcing hours and the top salary of 150 yen for female announcers. She was a Canadian Nisei.

There was Ruth Hayakawa who announced news on the hour, with commentary in the afternoon and evening, with a very low, resonant voice. She was born and raised in Japan, then educated in the U.S.

Then there was Fumy Saisho, also a native Japanese, distinctly feminine with a broad range of expression, who broadcast some of Radio Tokyo's most overt propaganda in English in a program, "The War As I See It" as Madame Tojo.

Teaming with Hayakawa in another heavy propaganda vehicle was Mieko Furuya, born in Los Angeles but now a citizen of Japan, on the English-language "Women's Magazine of the Air".

A dozen other women announced in English on Radio Tokyo, but these four combined the most natural English with the most experience – and all four were proven pro-Japanese. Any logical choice for the new Zero Hour announcer should have to come from among them.

When Cousens named Iva Toguri as his choice, Nakamoto was incredulous.

"Her voice is all wrong," he protested. "She's the wrong person."

"She's the one I want," said Cousens. "If it is your neck as well as mine, stay out of the way."

The order was given to the head of the personnel section, Shegecheka Takano, who informed Iva that she must take a voice test on that afternoon, the afternoon of November 10.

Iva was completely bewildered. She objected strongly. She never in her life had broadcast in a radio program and she never had fancied herself to be an announcer or an actress. Still protesting, she was led down to a ground floor studio, one of the very small ones – where Nakamoto, Cousens, and one of the guards were waiting for her.

Cousens took her aside, out of Nakamoto's hearing.

"Now, listen. This is a straight-out entertainment program. I have written it and I know what I'm doing. All you have to do is look upon yourself as a soldier under my orders. Do exactly what you are told. Don't try to do anything for yourself and you will do nothing that you do not want to. You will do nothing against your own people. I will guarantee that personally because I have written the script and I know what I'm doing."

The bewildered Iva was handed a script and the first program of the expanded Zero Hour went over the air from studio #5 on the second floor that night, at 6 p.m., Tokyo time.

Iva sat before a microphone looking into the control booth where Reyes spun a Boston Pops recording of "Strike up the Band" to open the show. Cousens read a few minutes of PW messages. She then heard him say the pre-arranged cue:

"Here comes your music."

The "On The Air" panel lit up and she was talking. She read announcements between records for 15 or 20 minutes and then her part was over. Ince followed with "Home Front New" – items monitored from broadcasts in the United States. Then Reyes took over with his announced "Original Zero Hour" – jazz records.

Iva followed Cousens into the PW room.

"This is crazy," she said. "I can't do this. I'm no good at it."

"You are just what we want," Cousens assured her. "We don't want an experienced announcer. We want a Yankee voice with a certain personality in it – a little touch of a WAC officer and a lot of cheer. I'll coach you to read the scripts the way I want them, so don't worry. You are just what we want."

He coached her daily after that, six days a week, on how to read the scripts which he wrote in longhand (Cousens couldn't type).

"Put yourself among the GIs in the South Pacific," he said. "You are with them, laughing with them, joking with them – getting them to sing along with your records. Always be cheerful. Always laugh when you say 'enemy'.

"Today you are reading a character patterned after the Japanese servant, Frank Watanabe in the 'Frank and Archie' series. Every Australian in the South Pacific will recognize it and so will a lot of Americans. It was recorded and first played in California."

Cousens dubbed Iva's broadcasting name as Orphan Ann and began writing it into the script.

For the first time since the beginning of the war Iva felt useful – felt that she was doing something for the American war effort under the very noses of the Japanese.

Iva quit Domei in December, after she learned that she could begin work as a secretary at the Danish legation in Tokyo in January, 1944. The new job placed her in pleasant and congenial surroundings for the first time since she had come to Japan. Everyone from Lars Tillitse, the Danish Minister, on down, was convinced that Japan would lose the war. Tillitse also received complete reports of allied news from diplomatic sources. Iva didn't have to sneak around now to obtain the news she gave to the prisoners. But, of course, she still had to transfer it to them secretly at Radio Tokyo.

About the time she went to work at the Danish legation, the PWs at Radio Tokyo gave her a purpose which took up all of her leisure time, much of her money, and a good share of her tenuous security as an alien resident of Japan.

Cousens and Ince were moved back to Bunka Prison on December 18, 1943, where they found that conditions were getting steadily worse. The men had scurvy, pellagra, and beri beri. Their rice rations and Red Cross packages were being stolen by their guards. The prisoners elected Cousens as their leader to attempt some way of obtaining food, especially citrus fruits, medicine (particularly quinine and vitamin pills), and tobacco. Cousens appealed to Iva.

She had been supplying food, medicine, and tobacco for Cousens, Ince, and Reyes since August – now she was asked to forage for a total of 27 PWs at Bunka.

All fruits and vegetables were scarce. Tobacco was rationed, and medicine was hard to find. Iva would scour drug stores and countryside and buy whatever was in season or in stock.

She got some fruits and vegetables from Felipe's grandmother's place in Atsugi. With the arrival of spring and summer in '44 she was able to buy tangerines, apples, and pears.

From farmers and neighbors she brought in weekly supplies of eggs, flour, rice, bread, sugar, and oatmeal.

She was able to get sugar from the Danish Minister, Tillitse, telling him it was for her own use. She also got matches from him. He was rationed these items as a member of the diplomatic corps. Rations of sugar and matches were not available to Japanese civilians or to aliens.

Iva got salt from Lily Sagoyan, whose father owned a bakery.

She also bought such items as she could get on the black market.

She obtained medicine chiefly in the form of yeast tablets or capsules, yeast oil tablets, quinine, aspirin, vitamin pills, or whale oil. Occasionally she would come across a drug store that had supplies of such items and she would buy all she could. She was able to buy some medicines from Dr. Omano. She also enlisted Felipe in her foraging efforts, and a young agricultural student, Harry Ito, who was able to bring in food from the country. On several occasions she pressed her friends, Ken Ishii and Charles Yoshii, into service as well.

For tobacco she would line up for hours to wait her turn; bought some on the black market, and occasionally got some from the Danish Minister.

Soap, also very scarce, came from the Danish residence, and she bartered it for food in the country.

Iva repaired clothing for the PWs, too. Through Cousens they sent out ragged coats, trousers, and sweaters. She repaired the tattered clothing, even sewing in double linings in the coats, and Cousens wore the repaired clothing back into Bunka.

Iva was thankful to be busy. The time went faster than it ever had since she had left the United States.

Meanwhile, Orphan Ann as Tokyo Rose had become a star.

CHAPTER VI

THE LAST DAYS OF RADIO TOKYO

The Orphan Ann broadcasts were heading into the most awesome military campaign ever mustered. Island by island, the Americans were preparing to move 4,000 miles across the Pacific to Japan. "Anyone who wants to know where we're going need only look at the map,' said Willis H. Hale, Commanding General of the 7th American Air Force.

First on the Gilberts, then the Marshalls, then the Marianas – convulsive land, air, and sea battles rages, lasting a few days or weeks – then, with the battles moving on, the islands subsided into the infinite quiet of the sky, the murmur of surf on smashed landing craft and subdued sand, the incredible beauties of Pacific sunrises and sunsets.

To the American pilots, the warm climate was wonderful, but contrasted with weather that was often treacherous, rapidly changing, with no dependable forecasts available; moving fronts reached altitudes too high to fly over, forcing pilots to fly just above the waves in driving rainstorms.

That vast area, until 1937, had existed to Americans as a movie hula scene, peopled by beautiful girls and pagan chiefs. That consciousness was shattered with the round-the-world flight of Amelia Earhart, who disappeared somewhere near uninhabited Howland Island on July 1, 1937. That disappearance brought on the greatest Naval search in history for an individual, carried out by both the United States and Japan, but for very different reasons – the Japanese were suspicious that she was in the Mandated Islands as a spy. However, after the searches were abandoned, any realistic grasp of that part of the world faded once again from the American national consciousness and never re-entered until late '43, almost the same time that home-front Americans started talking about Orphan Ann as Tokyo Rose.

As three million Americans started moving closer to Japan, Orphan Ann became the most popular Tokyo Rose. Orphan Ann never sang on the air, but she exhorted her listeners to do so. She made the focal transition for Tokyo Rose from news commentator to sing-along disc jockey, from propagandist and intelligence agent to playmate.

Excerpts from Orphan Ann's "Zero Hour" scripts, dated from February 22 to May 12, 1944, show the style that made her the most popular Tokyo Rose from Alaska clear around the Allied Pacific perimeter to Australia:

02/22/44

Hello there, enemies . . . how's tricks? This is Ann of Radio Tokyo, and we're just going to begin our regular program of music . . . news and the Zero Hour for our friends . . . I mean, our enemies! . . . in Australia and the South Pacific . . . So, be on your guard, and mind the children don't hear! All set? O.K., here's the first blow at your morale . . . the Boston Pops . . . playing 'Strike up the Band'. [1]

03/09/44

Thank you . . . thank you . . . thank you . . . Now then, stand by, the Orphan Choir! . . . this is Radio Tokyo calling and presenting our special program for listeners in Australia and the South Pacific. For the next 10 minutes we are going to listen to a superb presentation of the melodies of Stephen Foster . . . the performers are well know wandering minstrels, the Orphans of the South Pacific, supported by Nat Shilkret and the Victor Salon Group . . .

That's not bad atoll, atoll! . . . alright boys, one more lap, and then you can have your beer . . . what . . . no beer? Well, what sort of a war is this? Never mind, sing, first, and write to Ickes afterwards. Maybe he'll run a pipe for you . . sing, sing, little ones! [2]

03/10/44

And here it is! . . . Punctual . . . alert, and smiling . . . her radiant personality electrifying all those in the studio as she addressed herself to her vast worldwide audience . . . what's that you say? . . . Who is it? . . . Aw shucks! It's me of course . . . can't a girl give herself a little build-up when there's nobody else to do it? . . . you wait . . . you'll be sorry . . . In the meanwhile, you heartless wretches, here's Andre Kostelanetz playing 'The Chant of the Weed' . . . dope music to you! [3]

03/14/44

Thank you . . . thank you . . . Now just hold everything while I deal with these strangers . . . Hmm, this is Radio Tokyo calling, you are listening to a special program presented for the entertainment of our listeners in Australia and the South Pacific . . . there, that'll take care of them! . . . Now where was I? . . . Oh yes! . . . more memories for you,

Boys! . . . but listening music this time . . . So relax and please to listening, honorable boneheads! [(4)]

03/18/44

(Following 'London Bridge March' from Eric Coates London Suite)

Like that? . . . me too, but that Orphan Choir is a bit weak tonight, I could train a quartet of mosquitoes to do better than that! . . . let's try again, and then I hand you over to my learned colleagues who will present you news highlights and the Zero Hour! . . . Sing little ones! [(5)]

03/22/44

. . . Hello everybody! This is Ann of Radio Tokyo calling you with our regular program for listeners in Australia and the South Pacific. Did they look after you alright last night . . . while I was away? . . . I was hiking . . . No, not at night! . . . during the day . . . and you know how it is, don't you, my little Orphans of the South Pacific? . . . well, as one hiker to another, lets put our feet up and do some some listening. Some more of Eric Coates music tonight starting with the 'Dance in the Twilight' from his Springtime Suite. [(6)]

03/24/44

(Following 'Kreisleriana' and Rudy Vallee Tunes)

Not bad, not bad! . . . but now we're going to hear some real singing . . . Ladies and Gentlemen! . . . the Orphan Choir . . . for years, collectors have been touring the jungles and atolls of the South Pacific to collect these superb specimens of the celebrated featherless songster . . . the Singing Bonehead! . . . one more feather and he'd fly . . . as it is, he sings . . . Listen! [(7)]

03/25/44

(Gilbert and Sullivan selections)

Well, that got that over for a month or so I think, I hope! . . . Now let's do some singing . . . all ready the Orphans Choir? . . . well here's a light opera Company to help you with some musical comedy marches . . . after this one I hand you over for your news highlights and the Zero Hour . . . so sing nicely for mamma, little ones! . . . You be still, sergeant! [(8)]

03/27/44

Thank you . . . thank you . . . Greeting everybody!   This is your little playmate, I mean your bitter enemy, Ann, with a program of dangerous and wicked propaganda for my victims in Australia and the South Pacific . . . Stand by! You unlucky creatures . . . here I go! . . . Peter Dawson singing 'Ol Man River'

('Ol Man River)

See what I mean? . . . dangerous stuff, that . . . and it's habit forming, before you know where you are you're singing, too . . . and then where are you! . . .doggone it! . . . there's a war on isn't there? . . . so none of this singing nonsense . . . Sergeant! . . . gag those men, we're going to have some music . . . (9)

03/30/44

Sir, on behalf of the Union of Orphans of the South Pacific, I thank you! . . . Greetings everybody! . . . this is your enemy Ann calling you once again from Radio Tokyo with our special program for our friends in Australia and the South Pacific . . . tonight we open with selections from 'You're in Love' . . . a little hate propaganda composed by Friml and presented by the Victor Salon group! (10)

04/10/44

(After opening with 'Gypsy Love' and 'A Study in Blue')

This is Radio Tokyo's special program for listeners in Australia and my Boneheads in the South Pacific. Right now I'm lulling their senses before I creep up and annihilate them with my nail file . . . but don't tell anybody! . . . Now here's the next waltz I promised you, Victor Herbert's 'Kiss Me Again'. You heard me! (11)

04/21/44

Greetings everybody! Meet the girl who put the O in ptomaine! This is Ann back at the microphone and presenting Radio Tokyo's special program for listeners in Australia and the South Pacific. How's my orphan family, have you been good boys? . . .Alright, then, we'll have some music . . . a tango to start with . . . 'I Kiss Your Hand, Madame'.

(Program of tangos followed by home front news)

Thank you, thank you, thank you, and that brings us back to the music again . . . any latecomers listening? . . . Well, you're sharing Radio

Tokyo's regular program for Australia and the South Pacific . . . Dangerous enemy propaganda, so beware! Our next propagandist is Arthur Fiedler with the Boston Pops Orchestra playing Ketelbeys's 'In a Persian Market'. [12]

05/12/44

Who, me? . . . That's not a smile, my shoe's hurting! Hello everybody! . . . this is your little playmate Ann of Radio Tokyo presenting our usual nightly program for our friends in Australia and parts adjoining . . . How'd you like that? . . . 'Parts adjoining' . . . sounds kind of professional doesn't it? And after all what's a few hundred miles between friends? O.K. I heard you the first time! . . . but it's no good complaining now, honorable boneheads, so let's be cheerful and have some music . . .

('Strike up the band')

That's better! . . . now let's have some more of that close harmony work from the 'New Guinea Nightingales', and other chapters of the Pacific Orphans Choir. Here's some more Stephen Foster for you, so sing nicely, little ones . . . Jeep, Jeep! [13]

By mid-August, 1944, the "Boneheads" of Orphan Ann were making excellent progress. They had punched to within 1,500 miles of Japan from two directions: (1) from Midway to Saipan moving westerly and (2) from "down under" past the length of New Guinea moving north.

Army and Navy bombers were pounding Iwo Jima in the Volcano Islands, and Davao and Clark field in the Philippines. Giant B-29s had made their first appearances from Chinese bases over the mainland of Japan.

The notorious Zero fighter long before had lost its advantage to newer, more formidable American fighter planes such as the P-38, P-41, the Navy Wildcat, the Hellcat, the Chance-Vought Corsair, and now the P-51 Mustang.

Japan's most ingenious air leaders, Admiral Isoroku Yamamoto, and the two men considered the "brains" of the Japanese Naval Air Staff, Commander Toibana and Muroi, were dead – shot down by P-38s while on a tour of front line Japanese air bases along Bougainville's west coast.

Japan's initial force of front-line pilots who had delivered the bombs and torpedoes at Pearl Harbor and against the British and Dutch fleets in the South China Sea, were now down to a skeleton force. Their reinforcements were green recruits flying against prohibitive odds in favor of American armament, firepower, experience, and morale.

The "Turkey Shoot" at Saipan, in which 400 of 450 Japanese planes committed fell before American pilots and Navy gunners was the start of an aerial rout that was interrupted only briefly by the "kamikaze" missions.

The land forces which had pushed Japanese troops back 3,500 miles west of Midway – the First, Second, and Fourth Marine Divisions, the Seventh and Twenty-Seventh Infantry Divisions, the Seabees, and the veteran National Guard outfits in the South Pacific, were finally getting rotated home. A new crop of Americans were entering the Pacific to launch the final push – except for some few men such as John Basilone – the indomitable Marine sergeant who had won practically every combat medal the U.S. had to offer but still refused to go home.

At Radio Tokyo, Tsuneishi could see that his propaganda warfare never would have the effect he had hoped for. The winning side in a war is, essentially, impervious to propaganda. Only losers are subject to rapid psychological demoralization in combat.

Tsuneishi had allowed the Zero Hour to become primarily an entertainment program as listener bait so that he might have a wider audience at such times as the Allies suffered defeats or, if that failed to materialize, whenever the Japanese would put up sufficiently stern resistance to rattle their attackers.

As Tsuneishi explained it after the war:

"At that time (in autumn, 1944), Japan was suffering a speedy defeat, and so from my viewpoint it was satisfactory if we could produce any broadcasts that were then appealing, or would appeal to the GIs. But I figured that we would wait until the Japanese troops put severe resistance either in the Philippine Islands, in Okinawa, or on the mainland of Japan, and when they were thus separately resisting, then the program would continue. From that time the propaganda would be greatly increased. Until that time I felt it could be just a general appeal to the troops.

In my opinion, if the war had continued and if the Japanese had come to a position of stubbornly holding a line, either on the mainland of Japan or Okinawa or such places, and had this resulted in a considerable loss of lives to the American troop, had that been the case, then gradually on the mainland of America, more and more people would be saying that it would be well to end the war as soon as possible. At such a time, if stronger or more emphatic propaganda were broadcast, it would have considerable effect." [14]

As a new Tokyo Rose, Orphan Ann (with the possible exceptions of Madame Tojo, and Margie from Radio Manila), had become the most widely known "enemy" personality in the Pacific. Men speculated constantly about who she might be.

By the fall of 1944, however, there was an apparent change in Orphan Ann from earlier months of listening during the battles at Kwajalein and Eniwetok, back in the spring and early summer of '44. There now was a new escape tone. The music projected more of a dream quality, a "let's get away from it all" effect, and Orphan Ann now interjected into her usually cheerful comments such words as these:

"Things are bound to get better. The world is a little upside down . . . so let's forget the whole thing . . . let's forget with music." [15]

She began to call her "boneheads" "you fighting GIs", and when she said that she didn't laugh. Through it all was a consistent undertone of kinship. To anyone experienced in radio production and voice techniques, her intention was unmistakable – Orphan Ann projected herself as one of her listeners.

Certainly, the new Tokyo Roses had a vast audience. It was getting bigger all the time and it stretched from Kiska and Attu in the Aleutians throughout the Pacific to Northern New Guinea. Every man who entered the Pacific theatre had heard about Tokyo Rose and wanted to hear her broadcasts. But just as Ann's popularity reached its peak, the guiding talent that had created her left the show. PW writer/director Charles Cousens suffered nervous collapse and was hospitalized, leaving Orphan Ann as an orphan indeed.

At Radio Tokyo, many reports about the popularity of Tokyo Rose had filtered in and a number of the women announcers scented possible fame. Mieko Furuya and Mary Ishii made it clear that they would like to be on the Zero Hour. Both of them substituted for Iva when she was absent, as did Ruth Hayakawa, June Suyama, and Kay Fujiwara.

However, without Cousens to write the scripts, the quality of the program suffered. The American PW, Ted Ince, also disappeared from the Zero Hour for a time, but he came back in August – thinner, more embittered, but no less defiant. His return made the transfer of Allied news, food, tobacco, and medicines easier for Iva. She met him each Saturday afternoon on the stairway between the second and third floors for a covert transfer of supplies.

Ince asked her for a blanket for a sick man and she gave him one of only two woolen blankets in her possession. It was the only woolen blanket ever to appear among the prisoners at Bunka. The light covers provided by the Japanese were made of wood fiber.

Iva absented herself from Radio Tokyo more and more frequently. She spent two weeks in August at a mountain resort, Karuizawa, with the family of the Danish Minister, Lars Tillitse. That was a wonderful two weeks – away from Radio Tokyo – away from the war – away from everything.

She laid for long hours in the mountain stillness in complete solitude. She thought about quitting Radio Tokyo, and marrying Felipe. The two things had become linked in her mind but each would be a complicated step. Felipe was a Catholic and Iva a Methodist, but that wasn't the greatest difference between them. Iva was American and Felipe was Portuguese. Felipe argued that she never could go back to the states because of her role at Radio Tokyo, but Iva didn't believe that. She felt that she knew Americans better than he did, and she felt strongly that Americans would only laugh at what she had done to Japanese propaganda at Radio Tokyo.

In September, 1944, a loyalty check was in progress at Radio Tokyo. The atmosphere of defeat was causing a stricter point of view from the top down.

Iva was approached by a man wearing a trench coat as she started to enter the broadcasting studios on a September afternoon just before the Zero Hour program. She recognized that he was a friend, a former schoolmate of Felipe's, David Seizo Huga, who was now liaison man between Imperial Japanese Army Headquarters and civilian personnel at Radio Tokyo.

"Well, you are the last one," he said cheerfully.

"The last one?"

"Yes, the last member of the Zero Hour program. All the rest have agreed to cooperate with the army – now it's your turn."

"What do you mean?"

"The Army wants assurance that civilian employees will cooperate in case there should be any doubt about it."

"You will never get it from me."

Huga hurriedly cautioned her to speak softly and motioned her away from the studio door.

"Listen, this is Colonel Tsuneishi"s order (Tsuneishi had recently been promoted from Major to Lt. Colonel). All he is asking for is a verbal agreement. Now don't be foolish."

Iva shook her head.

"Things are going to tighten up – you must do this," Huga continued.

Iva's lips tightened.

Huga shook his head.

"I'll try to get you out of this, but if it doesn't work, you will hear about it."

However, Tsuneishi's attention was distracted by threats much more immediate and potent than the possible disloyalty of an American ex-patriot at Radio Tokyo. New American B-29 bombers had appeared over the Japanese for the first time on June 15th, the day before the U.S. launched its Saipan operation. Forty-seven of the big planes bombed the steel center at Yawata in Kyushu.

That was a severe blow to the homefront psyche so carefully preserved by Army propagandists at Radio Tokyo. The Doolittle raid of 1942 had been dismissed logically as a token affair, but the meaning of this B-29 raid was unmistakable. The Japanese homeland had finally come within range as a permanent target for U.S. bombers. These bombers would come back – more and more frequently and in greater numbers – and Japan had nothing in the air which could fly high enough, mount enough armor, or enough firepower to stop them.

On July 8th and August 11th, B-29s again flew from bases on the mainland of China to bomb southern Japanese cities. Five days later, on August 16th, two B-29s flew a reconnaissance mission from the opposite direction over the Bonin Islands. There was only one conclusion as to where that latest flight had originated – Saipan. This meant that the American B-29s could now reach Japan from the south. The next step for the American forces was the pork-chop shaped island of Iwo Jima – just halfway, 750 miles north of Saipan and 750 miles south of Japan.

The B-29s attacked from Chinese bases again on August 20th – 60 of them in a night raid. Then they temporarily vanished from the skies over Japan – reappearing next on October 30th over the island of Truk, the already neutralized Japanese Naval Base in the Carolines, far from any China air bases.

The American strategy became clear: the U.S. had evacuated its B-29 bases in China and had moved them to Saipan, and the next move to Iwo Jima would bring them easily within round-trip range of every major city in Japan. The Japanese High Command knew it, but they couldn't prevent it.

About 1:30 p.m. on November 1st, aircraft spotters sighted two of the giant American bombers flying high above Tokyo, lazily taking pictures out of range of interceptors. The first raid on Tokyo followed three and a half weeks later on November 24th – 60 B-29s bombed the Nakajima airplane works at Kichijoji, an engine factory. This raid caused heavy damage and killed or injured 260 people. But the full significance of what Tokyo was in for had not yet been realized. That came five days later, on November 29th.

This raid hit the heart of the city, igniting huge fires in Kanda and Nihonbashi, destroying 2,500 homes and rendering 15,000 homeless. For the first time, Tokyo residents knew the full meaning of fear from air attack. They were part of the target area. The Americans were after industrial plants and all of Tokyo-Yokohama was a single giant industrial complex.

The propaganda line at Radio Tokyo had become ludicrous. Iva no longer could doubt that GIs were laughing every time they heard news commentary by Oki or Nakamoto. When a country was being as obviously pummeled as Japan was, the only rational propaganda line was silence. But Nakamoto and Oki went for the grotesque line of "planned withdrawals" and bloated claims of sunken ships and downed aircraft.

One month prior to the first Tokyo raid, Iva had moved directly into the aerial "line of fire" so to speak – on October 26. She moved from Atsugi back to Tokyo proper, to Mrs. Unami Kido.s boarding house at 396 Ike Jiri Machi Setagaya-Ku. She made the move to cut expenses and to save time enroute to her jobs. The move cut her expenses by the 30 yen per month which she had been paying for train and streetcar fare from Atsugi. She now was spending between 50 and 80 yen per month on her aid to the PWs at Bunka – no one had shared the expenses with her (except Felipe d'Aquino) since Cousens had left Radio Tokyo.

The air raids occasionally interrupted transportation, giving her a new excuse for absences from the radio station.

The B-29s concentrated on night raids of Tokyo from early December, 1944 to early February, 1945. The city burned constantly, fed by the flimsy wooden and straw houses within the industrial areas. A funeral pyre of smoke hovered in the sky from dawn to dusk, and flames lit the night. The number of planes varied – 80 B-29s on December 3rd, 50 on December 27th, 75 on January 27th. But it was only the beginning.

On February 16th, three days before the invasion of Iwo Jima, one thousand American carrier-based planes swept over the Kanto area of Tokyo shooting at any vehicle that moved or any building which looked like it might produce something. The next day 600 planes returned to continue the attack in a morning and an afternoon raid. This was another numbing surprise for the population of Tokyo. They had expected carrier-based assaults – but not over Tokyo and certainly not in such numbers.

Radio Tokyo no longer had any practical propaganda function, but it continued to grind on. The kamikaze scare was about the only propaganda left to sell, and it was foolish to sell that because that would only make the enemy feel more justified with any measures he might take. Kamikazes were hardly an antidote for the awesome power then converging on Japan.

While the Iwo Jima fighting still raged early in March, 1945, B-29s began using the air strip there for emergency landings. That was all that Major General Curtis LeMay had been waiting for. Assured that attacking planes could get back at least to Iwo Jima, he unleashed his Twentieth Air Force in full strength for the first time on the Tokyo area.

On the nights of March 9th and 10th, a week before Iwo Jima was fully secured, 300 unarmed, stripped-down B-29s flew over Tokyo at a height of only 7,000 feet and dropped from six to eight tons of jelly-gasoline and fire bombs per plane.

At the time, Iva took her most prolonged absence from Radio Tokyo. She was taking religious instruction for her approaching marriage to Felipe d'Aquino in the Catholic Church of Father Kraus. The hiss of incendiaries and dazzling flash of jelly bombs was terrifying. The whole world seemed to have caught fire. Iva stayed in the house because she considered the air raid shelters as death traps. Incendiary fragments falling on rooftops rattled above and around her like "beans on tin".

American pilots reported that Tokyo "caught fire like a forest of pine trees".

Sixteen and a half square miles of the city burned that night and the next day as flames were whipped along by a brisk wind. The tower of the Diet building stood out black against an otherwise red sky. The city was as bright as sunrise with clouds of smoke and soot boiling across it. Japanese estimates of the dead ranged from 80 thousand to 300 thousand.

Iwo Jima was finally secured on March 16th. On April 7th, 108 Iwo Jima-based P-51 Mustang fighters of the Seventh Fighter Command raided Tokyo in low-level attacks. From that time on Japan was free game for anything which could mount guns and fly 1,500 miles in a round trip.

Iva stayed away from Radio Tokyo through all of March and April, 1945. She married Felipe on April 19th, thus becoming a Portuguese citizen. However, she would not renounce her American citizenship. She then received a postcard written in Japanese instructing her to return to work at Radio Tokyo, but she ignored it. Finally, a kempei agent came to forcefully assure her return. She went back to work early in May.

In her absence, Mieko Furuya (who had recently married Oki), June Suyama, Kay Fujiwara, and Mary Ishii had substituted for her.

The entire operation now seemed pointless to all concerned. Entertainment or propaganda in the midst of such devastation had become a mockery.

Tokyo became a nightmare of exploding bombs, burning rubble and bullet-racked ashes – with an occasional building skeleton rising from the ruin. After another awesome incendiary raid on May 25th and 26th, the American no longer considered Tokyo to be a worthwhile target.

About that time, Lt. Colonel Tsuneishi left Radio Tokyo, being re-assigned to the defense of the homeland. The Danish Ministry closed down, and Lars Tillitse left for Denmark – which ended Iva's job at the Danish legation.

Commerce was paralyzed in Tokyo – food became critically scarce.

In July of '45 the Japanese government ordered a ten per cent cut in the staple food ration – to a ration of 312 grams per adult per day of staple food, including substitutes. Famine was an immediate prospect for the coming winter.

Nevertheless, Iva continued her foraging for the PWs and maintained her weekly deliveries of food to Ince – that is, until her final broadcast on August 13th.

Even after the dropping of the bombs on Hiroshima on August 6th (78,150 killed) and on Nagasaki on August 9th (23,753 killed), the Zero Hour continued at Radio Tokyo like some senseless piper playing a grotesque tune in a crematorium.

Radio Tokyo finally shut down on August 15th – the day of the Japanese Surrender announcement by Emperor Hirohito.

Operation Zero Hour was finished, and would have sunk into eternal, well-deserved obscurity if it hadn't been for the legend of Tokyo Rose.

The legend was still very much alive and foremost in the minds of the American correspondents impatiently waiting at Okinawa for a plane ride to Japan.

CHAPTER VII

$2,000 FOR THE "ONE AND ONLY TOKYO ROSE"

For two weeks following the last broadcast at Radio Tokyo (on August 14, 1945), Iva sat in her tiny home in the burned-out rubble of Tokyo, awaiting the American occupation of the city, with far different feelings than those of her neighbors.

Her team had won, and she could hardly wait to celebrate the victory with other Americans. The opportunity to do that came much sooner than she expected.

On the evening of August 31st, just before any American troops had appeared in the city, one of Felipe's friends from Domei, Leslie Nakashima, rushed to her home with sensational news. Two American correspondents, he said, had offered $2,000 U.S. for Iva's exclusive story as Tokyo Rose, and they would be waiting for her with the money at the Imperial Hotel in the morning.

Iva could hardly believe her good luck. It was really over now – the poverty, the misery, the long exile from home. Two thousand dollars was a fortune in Japan. Her entire cumulative salary at Radio Tokyo for two years had amounted to less than $160. This $2,000 would mean passage money to the states and enough left over to help her father get a new start in business. And she would be able to tell her story of how the war prisoners and Orphan Ann had sabotaged Japanese propaganda at Radio Tokyo, right under the very noses of their captors.

Early the next morning, Iva dressed as she had for her weekend foraging trips into the countryside around Tokyo. She put on slacks, a blouse, a leather jerkin (jacket); then braided her hair in pigtails which she tied with a red ribbon. Then, she and Felipe and Les Nakashima hurried to the Imperial Hotel room of the two American correspondents.

When the door opened and she walked in, Iva received a shock.

Before her stood two men dressed like military officers, with a .45 revolver on a table beside a portable typewriter. The shades were drawn. Someone locked the door.

One of the pair was a dark-haired man, handsome and trim. The other was shorter, plumper, older, with an imperial-mustache, and beefy complexion. Iva was informed that the red-faced man was Harry T. Brundidge, associate editor for *Cosmopolitan* Magazine. The younger man was Clark Lee, world-famous correspondent for the International News Service.

Lee simply stared for a time. The shock was mutual.

From the first days of the war, which had caught him at Clark Field in the Philippines, Lee had heard many rumors about Tokyo Rose. He had heard that she was a stand-in for Amelia Earhart, trained to talk like her; or that she was Amelia Earhart herself; or that she was the wife of the special Japanese envoy to Washington (Kurusu); or that she was a St. Louis woman; or a hula girl from Maui, now become Tojo's mistress. At no time had he pictured her as anything like the pig-tailed young woman standing before him. She looked like an undernourished high school girl.

The air of secrecy and the presence of the revolver made the visitors clearly nervous. But after a few pleasantries, Iva sat down and read a one-page contract offered to her by Brundidge. Surely enough, it offered her $2,000 for the exclusive rights to her story as "the one and only Tokyo Rose". [1]

All signed the one-page contract, Nakashima left, and soon, Iva was talking freely and laughing about how the war prisoners had made a mockery out of the Zero Hour propaganda. Then, she sobered and, as she started to recall the circumstances of her trip to Japan, Lee began to type. She talked steadily and Lee typed for a couple of hours – until she told of the time when she started broadcasting in November, 1943.

Lee paused. If that date were true, then this woman could not be "the one and only Tokyo Rose". Lee remembered that the men on Bataan early in 1942 had been talking about Tokyo Rose. Lee said nothing about that to Iva, however.

They broke for lunch in the room and continued typing until the afternoon.

According to what Iva was telling him, Lee surmised that she had been a one-woman USO, broadcasting to boost Allied morale under the direction of war prisoners.

By about three o'clock, Lee had 17 pages of double-spaced notes. Lee got up and stretched. His impression was that he had just heard one of the war's biggest cock-and-bull stories. The part about the prisoners getting her to broadcast was bad enough, but the topper was the baloney about having supplied the PWs with food, drugs, Allied news, and tobacco – under the noses of the secret police at Radio Tokyo for two years.

Blithely ignorant of Lee's negative thoughts, Iva left without a care in the world, still dreaming of a quick return home, and reunion with her family.

"It never entered my mind – I never dreamed that my conduct could be in any way interpreted as wrong." Iva recalled. *"I was not aware of any need for a lawyer. Why should I need a lawyer? I felt there was no need to be reserved. I answered all of their questions truthfully.*

"As the interview progressed, I increasingly realized they were off on a tangent. When Brundidge or Lee (I don't remember which) asked me if I had made statements referring to troop and ship movements and 4Fs out with soldiers, it came to me as a surprise. But I saw no threat in that. I had never dealt in information about troop movements and didn't fully comprehend the idiomatic meaning of 4F in the States. I certainly never had used the term in a broadcast."

"I left the room with no sense of uneasiness," she remembered later, *"If I had been impressed with some threat growing out of that interview, I would have contacted a lawyer. I didn't"* [2]

After she had left, Lee wrote his story first, then tossed the notes to Brundidge.

Lee's byline sped to California via cable that night, and the next day Tokyo Rose was on the front page, with Iva Toguri named as a traitor:

From the Los Angeles Examiner, September 3, 1945:

"TRAITOR'S PAY—TOKYO ROSE
GOT 100 YEN A MO. - - - $6.60"

by Clark Lee

(Staff correspondent for INS)

"Tokyo, Japan (Delayed) – The one and only 'Tokyo Rose', a Los Angeles   born American of Japanese ancestry is 'willing to take her medicine'.

"But Iva Ikuko Toguri . . . does not feel that she was a traitor to the U.S.

"For the job of trying to make American troops homesick she was paid a miserable 100 yen monthly – $6.60 at the present exchange rate.

"In an exclusive interview with this correspondent, Iva admitted she did not think it through when she took the job, nor did she consider the possibilities of being adjudged a traitor to her country.

"She said she believed Americans would enjoy her music and laugh at her propaganda . . ." [3]

Brundidge then designed his own 5,000 word story for *Cosmopolitan* as a first-person confession of treason, as acknowledged by Iva Toguri, told to Harry Brundidge. He sent his story to Frances Whiting, editor of *Cosmopolitan* Magazine, New York.

That night Brundidge savored his triumph, and anticipated the $2,000 he would need to fulfill his part of the contract with Iva Toguri.

The next morning he received the shock of his life. A cablegram informed him that his editor, Frances Whiting, did not want the exclusive confessions of Tokyo Rose! Further, a copy of her cablegram had been posted on a bulletin board at Atsugi Air Base so that all 300 of Brundidge's rival correspondents in the race for Tokyo Rose might enjoy it. Brundidge exploded. Storming about like a madman, he raged to Clark Lee:

"She rejects it . . . the most sensational story in occupied Japan . . . and she rejects it! That . ." He was reduced to sputtering.

One compelling thought then haunted Brundidge's pounding head. He had a $2,000 contract to pay and nothing to pay it with. He was in trouble.

Brundidge then hurried to the Eighth Army CIC offices of General Willard Thorpe and urged the arrest of Iva Toguri as Tokyo Rose.

"She's a traitor," he said, "and there's her confession." He then tossed the 17 pages of news notes typed by Lee. To absolve himself from the terms of payment in the contract, he suggested a mass news conference.

Next day, a lieutenant and a sergeant in an Eighth Army jeep halted before Iva Toguri's small house. They arrested her, and drove her to the Bund Hotel in Yokohama.

"It seemed like there were correspondents hanging from the rafters," Iva recalled. "They were all over the place. I didn't sense any hostility – just curiosity. Everybody just stared. There was a big silence when I walked in, but people were relaxed and informal – all were in some kind of uniform. Then, after the Bund Hotel meeting and pictures with General Eichelberger, they put me under hotel arrest for the night, at the New Grand, but everything was so jovial that it all seemed a big joke." [4]

She was back to her house in Tokyo the next day.

At the Eighth Army CIC headquarters, Harry Brundidge turned in his copy of the exclusive contract with "the one and only Tokyo Rose". [5] Because Iva had shared her story with other correspondents, he said, the exclusive clause was broken.

None of the money was ever paid.

The U.S. Justice Department wired General Douglas MacArthur on October 18th:

"TAKE IVA TOGURI INTO CUSTODY FOR
INVESTIGATION OF TREASON CHARGES"

With her freshly-washed hair blowing in the wind, wearing slacks, and packing only her hastily-grabbed toothbrush, Iva Toguri was whisked away in a jeep to Yokohama Prison. She still hadn't contacted a lawyer.

At the prison, GIs stared at her in slack-jawed amazement. "This is Tokyo Rose?" their faces seemed to ask.

"I think they were expecting a combination of Ava Gardner and Anna Mae Wong," said Iva, *"and what they got was me."*

She got no sleep for the first three nights because of the constant stream of GIs and their friends past her cell.

"They took us out at 10 o'clock every day for a walk," she recalled, *"I hadn't even made my bed. I told Colonel Hardy, the prison C.O, why I hadn't. 'I haven't been able to sleep in it for the last three nights because of the constant procession.' He stopped it then, except for the high rankers..*

"Most of the GIs would just come and stare and leave. I don't know how they got in there. There were 17 gates – or something like that – between my cell and the outside.

"I was questioned about having dinner with Tojo – asked to acknowledge my help in shaping Japanese propaganda and policies. They wanted to know whether I could give them the reaction of Japanese officials to leaflets dropped from American planes. I never had seen any leaflets.

"Sometimes I was treated as a Japanese national, sometimes as an American citizen. The last straw (if you'll pardon the pun) was when they wanted me to sleep on a mat. There was a big deal about whether I should get Japanese food or American food (after all that I'd been through trying to avoid Japanese food, first at my uncle's place, and later, at the boarding house). Some thought I should get Japanese cigarettes and some, American cigarettes. I kept repeating, 'I'm an American, I tell you, I never set foot in Japan till I was twenty-five.' But it didn't do any good. They thought I was the world's biggest liar."

To her interrogators, the prisoner's account of her life in wartime Japan was inconceivable.

Meanwhile, the weeks sped by and the holiday spirit prevailed in the Christmas season among the occupiers in Tokyo. With the novelty gone from the Tokyo Rose situation, and some knotty legal contradictions to be untangled before anyone could make sense of the case, Iva's captors simply forgot about her.

After six weeks at Yokohama Prison, Iva was transferred to Sugamo Prison in Tokyo.

"At Sugamo, we could take a bath, whereas I had only one bucket of hot water for a bath at Yokohama. In fact, you had to manage a sponge bath and do your own laundry out of that one bucket of water. I got pretty good at it. Finally, I even had water left over. One gets into a situation where he looks forward to a bucket of water as the day's high point.

"There was no activity whatsoever as far as my case went. It seems like there's a blank from November 16, 1945 to February 1, 1946, when I saw Frederick Tillman (FBI Agent), but that's impossible. It seemed there were days and months when nothing happened."

The Japanese knew little about the American preoccupation with Tokyo Rose, and understood even less. When high-ranking Japanese were questioned about Tokyo Rose, they assumed that the interrogators suspected Japanese military authorities had something to do with a possible execution of Amelia Earhart; that the occupiers had war crime trials in mind. The Americans, in turn, thought that the Japanese played dumb about an actual broadcaster who had access to top military secrets concerning American troop movements, bombing targets, and the like.

CHAPTER VIII

SO . . . WHATEVER HAPPENED TO MYRTLE ?

The Eighth Army had everything it needed to find out what Iva Toguri d'Aquino had actually broadcast, including recordings of broadcasts by Iva Toguri or her substitutes (mainly Ruth Hayakawa, June Suyama, and Mieko Furuya) as Orphan Ann. The war prisoners who had broadcast with her were also available. The Zero Hour supervisors, Nakamoto, Mitsushio, and Oki, still lived in Tokyo. So did the ex-military boss of Radio Tokyo, Lt. Colonel Tsuneishi. But in the interrogations and psychological examinations of Iva Toguri at Yokohama and Sugamo, no clear line was being drawn between the actual broadcasts of "Orphan Ann", and other broadcasts at Radio Tokyo, or of broadcasts from other Japanese radio stations, nor the long history of stories and rumors that had combined to form the legend of Tokyo Rose.

"We were all run of the mill," said Iva, speaking of the women who had broadcast at wartime Radio Tokyo, *"not a glamor girl in the bunch."*

From Mary Ishii, who didn't look oriental (one parent was Japanese, the other English, and she could get lost in any crowd) to "Mother" Fayvelle Topping (the 83-year-old American missionary), all twelve Radio Tokyo Roses tended to sound better than they looked.

Meanwhile, investigators had easy access to the answer as to where the sexiest propaganda actually broadcast in the Pacific had come from – including the daily blasts about war workers and 4Fs who were stepping out with the wives of fighting GIs – and about dying horribly and needlessly in disease infested jungles and rotten foxholes. A beautiful woman had made them. She had sung torch songs, as well. And no one had to make a lengthy investigation to find out about her. All that one had to do was read *Yank Magazine*. It was all there, along with a big picture of that truly beautiful woman covering half of the front page, in the June 29 edition of 1945. [1]

She was the irrepressible Myrtle "Your Little Margie" Lipton of Radio Manila – a rare beauty. Myrtle was the only "Tokyo Rose" who came on the microphone drunk and indulged in wild, off-the-script stories and images..

Pictured in *Yank* Magazine of June 29, '45 from the waist up, Myrtle's large brown eyes and pert nose were framed in lovely curves and golden brown hair. Her mouth was full and untouched by makeup. Makeup could have done nothing to improve Myrtle. The eagerness of the interviewer, Sgt. Ozzie St. George, was equaled by Myrtle's responsiveness. She frequently volunteered answers before he could ask the question. Yes, she smoked and drank, said Myrtle; did Correspondent Ozzie have anything with him?

"Were you pro-Japanese or pro-American?" asked St. George.

"Neither," answered Myrtle, "I am pro-Filipino."

He had heard her program, "Memory Lane," said the interviewer, and Myrtle was delighted.

"I'm so glad," she said, "did you like it?"

She was paid 230 Japanese pesos per month, and the rest of her salary was in rations – rice, fish, soap, matches, sugar, and so on.

"My program was not a propaganda broadcast,' explained Myrtle. "It was just entertainment – just something to remind the fellows on New Guinea about the places back home."

No Allied war prisoners were used at Radio Manila, said Myrtle.

"There were always Japs around – civilians, but they carried guns and swords." Myrtle had three different supervisors. One pushed her around a little when she suggested that he slice rice cakes with his sacred Samurai blade, but generally Myrtle got along with them.

The first one, Ohmura, "wasn't such a bad old guy," said Myrtle. Ohmura first introduced her to her radio audience as Mary, but Myrtle forgot and signed off as Myrtle. Ohmura gave up the Mary idea and his star's broadcast name remained Myrtle until the Americans landed at Leyte. Then her radio name was changed to Margie.

Ohmura suggested that Myrtle listen to Tokyo Rose and model her program accordingly, because Rose's technique was "so appealing to the Americans," wrote St. George, but the *Yank* writer didn't specify who he thought Tokyo Rose was, or specify which Radio Tokyo program..

Myrtle remembered one specific quotation from her programs with Ohmura: "Those crisp football afternoons back home . . . Jim and Ann in Jim's Ford . . . I understand Ann finally married George . . . she didn't think Jim ever was coming home."

Myrtle said that Ohmura got fired when she played the Notre Dame Fight Song after an Allied victory had been announced over Radio Manila, but Myrtle continued to star, and script writer Ken Murayama (not to be confused with AP's Tamotsu Murayama), then rose to become Myrtle's director.

Ken described Myrtle as "a very good voice . . . quite low-pitched, husky . . . a torch singer . . . her English was very good." [2]

His scripts for Myrtle, said Ken Murayama, "were designed to create a sense of homesickness among the troops fighting in the Southwest Pacific. The tone was one of trying to make the soldiers recall certain good times they might have had when they were back in the States . . . We had stories, short scripts shall we say, of girls having dates with men at home, while possibly their sweethearts or husbands were fighting in the Southwest Pacific.

"I can't give you any exact quotations regarding malaria or jungle rot, but I am sure some of the scripts must have included diseases which were prevalent in the tropical areas . . . we relied heavily on waltzes – music which tended to be dreamy, usually old pieces. I believe the program came on with the playing of 'Auld Lang Syne' . . . We had some other signature number. I believe 'Aloha' was in it."

Did Myrtle ever come to the station intoxicated before her broadcasts? asked his questioner.

"Yes, several times," answered Murayama, and "she did a very good job."

Myrtle's third script writer and sometimes supervisor was George Kazumaro (Buddy) Uno. [3] When Myrtle was mentioned, Uno bubbled over.

"I thought her program was wonderful – it carried a punch – it was sexy – she had everything right for the program . . .

"This girl was a drinking girl, and sometimes she would come to the station at the last minute pretty well messed up, and she would say, 'I can take care of myself' and Ken would be there too, and would hand her the script and she would give off pretty much like a professional announcer, and all of a sudden she would lose control of herself and . . well . . she was reading something that was plain imagination . . but anything she did was very effective. She painted horrible pictures of jungles, dropping bombs, and foxholes. Then, she described the 'good old days' back home, saying things like 'what a pity you fellows have to die in the jungles without even knowing what you are fighting for'."

When Sgt. Ozzie St. George tried to reach Myrtle for a second interview, Myrtle had vanished, and word came back to St. George that Myrtle had died.

But Myrtle had not died. What actually happened to her remains a secret unrevealed. Myrtle, it is known, was investigated by the U.S. Eighth Army CIC Headquarters in Manila, immediately after the war, and received protective custody under one or more investigating officers She has never been heard from or of since.

CHAPTER IX

THE NONTRIAL

In the daily interrogations of Iva Toguri as Tokyo Rose at Sugamo Prison by FBI Agent Fred Tillman, he remembers, mostly, annoyance.

"She wouldn't keep her mouth shut," he said, "She was always cracking wise. I got tired of that.

"Of course, it isn't the interrogator's job to recommend for or against a trial. That decision had to made in the Justice Department. My job was to find out what had happened and give a report of it." [1]

"Usually," Iva remembered Tillman's interrogations, *"we started around 8 or 9 in the morning, and it lasted till 5. I suppose he was weary. I know I was weary. I suppose, toward the end, we were both sitting on a pincushion. The thing that provoked me most was that he kept on insisting I was lying – hiding something. I suppose they are trained that way. It got to where I just didn't give a damn. I was just weary of him and his endless questioning."*

Legally, the Justice Department was ill-equipped to go into a Tokyo Rose trial.

The United States has no law addressing crimes of collaboration. Under U.S. law, it was treason or nothing for a person in Iva Toguri's situation. The all-encompassing treason law as defined in the U.S. Constitution, circa 1789, Article IV, Section I, title 18:

"Whoever owing allegiance to the United States, levies war against them or adheres to their enemies, giving aid and comfort within the United States or elsewhere, is guilty of treason." [2]

As of 1946, only the English had found anyone guilty of treason for radio broadcasting, and the English trials had allowed for degrees of guilt. For eight of the Radio Berlin broadcasters, the English invoked a law amounting to collaboration, an offense against the National Defense Act. The sentences for the Radio Berlin broadcasters convicted under that charge ranged from two to ten years.

However, under the British Treason Act of 1351, which simply forbids any British subject to adhere to the King's enemies during "an open and public war", [3] James Joyce (Lord Haw Haw) and three others (John Amery, Walter Purdy, and Peter Haller Cooper) received death sentences. The sentences of Purdy and Cooper were commuted to life imprisonment, but Joyce and Amery were hanged.

In the matter of intent, Lord Haw Haw had put the noose firmly around his own neck. He had begun his book, *Twilight Over England*, with a sober acknowledgement: "Since I began these broadcasts, I have committed treason every day." The prosecution had only to take him at his word.

There were a total of six Americans whom the U.S. Government was considering for indictment for "treason by radio" at this time. All except Iva had been involved with broadcasting within the European Theatre. One was also a female, Mildred (Axis Sally) Gillars. The others were Douglas Chandler, Martin James Monti, Robert Best, and Ezra Pound But the U.S. Government, as yet, had made no move to try any of them.

Compared to the broadcasting by collaborators that had gone on in Berlin, the doings at Radio Tokyo didn't amount to much.

Further, in contrast to the heavy punishment dealt to British traitors and collaborators at Radio Berlin, the dozen or so men who had broadcast at Radio Tokyo went untried. [4] Cousens, never formally tried for treason, underwent a lengthy hearing by an Australian Court Martial and was freed after 22 days.

Such were the factors working against a treason trial for Iva Toguri d'Aquino as she languished at Sugamo Prison in 1946.

Meanwhile, her personal tragedy had deepened. Via the Red Cross, she received the first letter from her family since the first days of the war. It was from her brother, Fred, and had been written a long time before. It bore the news that Iva's mother had died in an Assembly Center for Japanese Americans at Tulare, California, in May, 1942. [5]

This was her first real confirmation that her family, among almost all other Japanese-Americans living in the western states in the aftermath of the bombing of Pearl Harbor, had been "interned" by the U.S. government into what amounted as prisoner-of-war camps. Iva still did not comprehend what this really meant, nor did she want to believe it.

The most ludicrous investigation of all occurred in July of '46. A party of U.S. Congressmen conducted a peeping-tom act on Iva as she took a shower at Sugamo Prison. Sergeant Martin Prey, the jailer, chased them away and wrote a letter of protest to the commanding officers of the prison. [6]

"They actually came to the shower door," said Iva, *"stuck their noses through the door – there were 16 or 17 of them. I could see the reflection of their faces in the smoky, milk-colored glass. I couldn't believe it!"*

Finally, following a year of imprisonment, the Justice Department ordered Iva Toguri released.

Behind the scenes, here's what happened:

The U.S. Attorney in Los Angeles, James M. Carter, sent a wire to Attorney General Tom Clark, Department of Justice in Washington D.C., on September 13th, 1946, stating:

"FURTHER INVESTIGATION MENTIONED IN CORRESPONDENCE HAS NOT STRENGTHED THIS CASE PD WE FEEL EVIDENCE INADEQUATE PD RECOMMEND TREASON PROSECUTION BE DECLINED PD END." [7]

In an office memorandum from Nathan T. Elliff, Chief, Internal Security Section, The Justice Department, to Theron L. Caudle, Assistant Attorney General, Criminal Division, The Justice Department, Ellif cited Carter's opinion and added:

"We concur in his opinion and suggest that this matter be considered closed at this time, and the War Department be advised that we no longer desire that the subject be retained in custody." [8]

Caudle then passed the recommendation for Iva's release to Attorney General Tom Clark, emphasizing the following points:

". . no broadcaster over Radio Tokyo was announced as 'Tokyo Rose' and . . . several women announcers of programs of this type were given that name indiscriminately by the American troops . ."

". . It appears that the identification of Toguri as 'Tokyo Rose' is erroneous, or, at least, that her activity consisted of nothing more than the announcing of musical selections."

"A few recording cylinders of her broadcasts and a large number of her scripts were located, and they . . . do not disclose that she did anything more than introduce musical records. In addition, it appears that 'Tokyo Rose' was broadcasting prior to the date of Iva Toguri's employment."

"It is my opinion that Toguri's activities, particularly in view of the innocuous nature of her broadcasts, are not sufficient to warrant her prosecution for treason." [9]

The arrangements were set at night, to keep the publicity down, but on the night of October 25, 1946, when Iva emerged from the series of corridors leading to the outside of Sugamo Prison, it might as well have been high noon. Every correspondent in the Far East seemed to have been tipped off. Waiting for her were newsmen from French papers, Australian papers, Reuters, INS, AP, UP, Domei, and Tass.

A platoon of soldiers formed double ranks. Through the ranks, in honor-guard style, Iva was escorted on the arm of the prison commander, Colonel Hardy, who presented her with a bouquet of roses.

At the end of the walk, she faced a barrage of press questions. She froze like a target caught in a searchlight. Then, a small, neatly-dressed man with impeccable manners somehow appeared beside her.

"Look," said the man, "do you want to get away from this?"

"Who are you," she demanded.

"I'm John Rich, of INS."

"INS!" she recoiled. "Get away from me. I don't want anything to do with INS."

"I don't blame you," said John Rich, "but I don't want a story. I want to offer you a cottage that INS maintains for retreats on Enoshima. You can stay there while the story cools off."

John Rich was saying, very plainly, that the correspondents of INS who knew what had happened to her were sorry about the company she had fallen into in that first interview at the Imperial Hotel.

The d'Aquinos went to the cottage on Enoshima and John Rich, true to his word, wrote nothing about it.

The Associated Press apparently put the wrap-up on the Tokyo Rose matter with a statement from the U.S. District Attorney's office in Los Angeles::

"Los Angeles, Ca., Oct 21 (AP) -- Because Tokyo Rose was a 'composite person with at least a dozen voices', the Federal Government today dropped its plan to prosecute Iva Ikuko Toguri on charges of dispensing subversive propaganda in the South Pacific during the war.

"Iva . . . occasionally broadcast programs beamed to American troops, But, said U.S. Attorney James M. Carter in dropping the case, 'Many other women in the broadcasting studio where she was employed as a stenographer also announced programs.'" [10]

That, apparently, was the end of any Tokyo Rose treason investigation.

Or, at least it would have been, if Harry Brundidge had not been so determined to sell his story of how he had trapped America's first woman "traitor". [11]

CHAPTER X

EXPOSE

"Good evening, Mr. and Mrs. America and all the ships at sea: let's go to press . . . Flash! . ."

So began the most popular radio news show in America in the year 1947, featuring the staccato voice of Walter Winchell, punctuated by the insistent beeping of a telegrapher's key. It was heard nationally every Sunday evening.

Walter Winchell was a gossip columnist for the New York *Evening Graphic* and *Daily Mirror* and a right-wing radio commentator, later to become aligned with Senator Joseph McCarthy's "Red Scare" campaign against communism.

"He wrote," said Ben Hecht, "like a man honking his horn in a traffic jam."

New Yorker Magazine once analyzed 239 column items by Winchell and proclaimed that 186 of them were "partly inaccurate, totally inaccurate, and/or unverifiable." [1] Winchell, it was revealed, had no real incentive to be accurate, because for most of his career his contract with his newspaper and radio employers required them to reimburse him for any damages he had to pay, should he be sued for slander or libel.

In the fall of 1947, as Iva Toguri renewed her efforts in Tokyo to obtain a U.S. passport and a passage back home, Winchell pressed hard for indictments of suspected WWII traitors, especially a trial against "Axis Sally" and "Tokyo Rose". He accused Attorney General Tom Clark and the Truman administration of being "soft on the traitors". [2] He argued that the Republicans would benefit tremendously in the coming 1948 presidential election if something were not done immediately to bring about treason trials of Tokyo Rose and Axis Sally.

On October 24th, the assistant U.S. Attorney General, T. Vincent Quinn, wrote to the office of the Secretary of State in a letter stating:

"Attention: R.B. Shipley, Chief, the Passport Division:

"After a careful analysis of the available evidence, the Department concluded that prosecution of this individual was not warranted, and we so informed the War Department. Therefore,

this Department will have no objection to the issue of a passport for Mrs. d'Aquino." [3]

Winchell, who broadcast with excited passion, was angry because the Truman administration was about to clear the way for Iva's return home, and broadcast vehemently against the issuance of a passport for her..

The Assistant U.S. Attorney General's opinion then seemed to have somehow become reversed, according to an article which appeared in the *New York Times* on December 3rd. The article stated that Iva Toguri would not be allowed to return to the States and asked for witnesses against her to communicate with the FBI. The headline article read:

"SEEK TREASON WITNESSES"

"Washington, Dec. 3 -- Anyone who ever saw Iva Ikuko d'Aquino broadcasting as 'Tokyo Rose' or recognized her voice coming over the air waves, should communicate with the FBI, that agency stated today.

". . Investigation for two years with a view of obtaining . . two witnesses   necessary to prosecute her for treason had thus far been unsuccessful.

"Nevertheless, said the FBI, the inquiry was proceeding and, if possible, the case would be presented to a grand jury. Meanwhile, Mrs. d'Aquino 'is not being permitted' to return to the U.S. at this time" [4]

On the next day, December 4th, 1947, in an attempt to placate the wrath of Walter Winchell with the U.S. Attorney General Tom Clark, District Attorney James M. Carter took a copy of the article and went to see Winchell in Los Angeles. Carter wrote later to U.S. Attorney General Clark, describing what transpired in his meeting with Winchell.

"I stated to Mr. Winchell," wrote Carter, "that there were about six women who broadcast from Radio Tokyo, only one of whom was an American citizen, to-wit, Iva Toguri. Winchell said he knew the facts . .

"Winchell made the following point:

"That it was the duty of the Attorney General and the Department of Justice to propose legislation to be used against such persons as 'Tokyo Rose',   and 'to do something about it'.

". . . I exhibited to him a copy of the press release in Washington concerning 'Tokyo Rose' and told him it was a complete copy of the release. He read it with interest, and stated he was glad to see that 'Tokyo Rose' was not to be allowed to come back to the United States; he intimated he was going to use the release, or part of it, on his Sunday night broadcast. He commented that the release did not say that it had been brought around by his previous broadcast.

"I repeated that I was not defending 'Tokyo Rose' and wished him more power in his activities in exposing American citizens who engaged in harmful and unpatriotic conduct, at home and abroad, but stated that as a lawyer I was not going to recommend a prosecution unless we had some kind of a case against the defendant.

"Mr. Carr (Charles Carr, formerly U.S. District Attorney in Los Angeles) had mentioned letters he had received as U.S. Attorney from governments from all over the world, criticizing Mr. Carr for his announced intention of prosecuting 'Tokyo Rose' and claiming that the 'Tokyo Rose' broadcasts, instead of being morale breakers, were morale builders. Winchell replied that these people were probably communists . . .

"I explained to him the innocuous character of the 'Orphan Ann' broadcasts, and offered to exhibit to him transcriptions of the 'Orphan Ann' broadcasts which were put out over the air by Iva Toguri. He stated that he was familiar with the fact that many of them were innocuous.

"I received . . . the impression that somewhere along the line his pride had been injured, and I am of the opinion that you could go a long way toward smoothing things out, should you have a personal chat with Mr. Winchell.

"As we left Mr. Winchell's office to go to our cars, the question of 'Tokyo Rose' came up again, and I suggested to him the bad situation which would occur should the Government seek a prosecution without having a proper case, and if the trial resulted in a dismissal or acquittal. He agreed readily that this would be worse than having no prosecution, and we parted in a very friendly manner." [5]

Harry Brundidge had read the December 3rd *New York Times* headline article, and saw renewed opportunity to sell his version of the 1945 interview with Iva Toguri as a "confession" by Tokyo Rose. On December 10th, Brundidge met with an FBI agent, Kline Weatherford, at his Mayflower Hotel room in Washington, D.C.

Weatherford read the seventeen pages of interview notes (originally written by Clark Lee) which Brundidge was calling a confession, but made no decision about them. He would get back to Brundidge on the matter, Weatherford said.

It became obvious that the way for the Truman Administration to counteract Winchell's and the GOP's charges that they were "soft on traitors" would be to stage a trial or two – preferably two – one for the Pacific and the other for the European theatre of operations. Two such trials would tap deep into the emotional war roots of just about everyone of legal voting age in the United States. The flavor of American opinion at the time was highlighted by a mixture of passionate patriotism, a fervor to seek-out World War II traitors, and strong anti-Japanese feelings – and 1948 was election year.

After the New Year holidays, Brundidge still had heard nothing from his meeting with Weatherford. He called upon Clark Lee, who had recently married Hawaiian Princess Liliuokalani Kahananakoa. Walter Winchell also made a call to Lee. On January 8th (1948), he quoted Lee as saying that the Justice Department's ad for eye witnesses to broadcasts by Tokyo Rose was a "cynical evasion".

> "Lee says nearly two years ago he turned over to FBI agents (in New York City) the original of an 18-page typewritten confession dictated to him by Tokyo Rose . . . 'Surely,' he writes, 'this document must be available to the State Department and Attorney General Clark'.

> "Lee certifies that she named two witnesses against her who would be easily available, 'if they really want to bring her to trial' . . . one witness was Lt. Ted Ince (alias Wallace) of the U.S. Army . . . The other was Major Cousens of Australia." [6]

Then, Winchell wrote a follow-up item, lamenting a supposed theft of the "confessions" from Harry Brundidge.

> *"When Clark Lee of INS (who got the 18-page confession dictated by Tokyo Rose, which was stolen later from colleague Harry Brundidge. Oh, Harry!) returned to the U.S. . . . "* [7]

Winchell managed to create a running story about the whereabouts of the "confession", and he kept the pattern going. Winchell then broadcast that Brundidge actually still had the confession – that it was the contract with Iva Toguri as "the one and original Tokyo Rose" that was "stolen", not the confession. Winchell then advised Brundidge on the air to turn the confession over to the FBI.

Then, according to Brundidge, he and the publisher of the *Nashville Tennesean*, Silliman Evans, and U.S. Attorney General Tom C. Clark met at the Mayflower Hotel in Washington, where Brundidge quoted Attorney General Clark as saying "Do something. We've got to get that fellow, Winchell, off our backs". [8]

The Republican "soft on traitors" charge was forcing Attorney General Tom Clack to reconsider his stance regarding "Tokyo Rose" and "Axis Sally" (Mildred Gillars)

Then something else had happened . . . a sort of grass roots movement against Iva Toguri had emerged.

Having applied for readmission to the United States shortly after her release from Sugamo Prison in 1946, she had drawn fire from two organizations as being unworthy to reenter the U.S.

First, there had been a resolution sent to the U.S. Secretary of State, to the National American Legion Headquarters, and to the California American Legion Headquarters, saying that the El Centro American Legion Post did not want Iva Toguri back in the U.S., or in Imperial County. [9] Iva had attended grammar school at Calexico in Imperial County.

A national American Legion representative then had called upon the Justice Department to expedite prosecution of Iva Toguri, saying that if she were granted unrestricted re-entry to the U.S., the action would "arouse the righteous indignation of the American people". [10]

In a subsequent resolution, the Los Angeles city council passed a hometown rejection of any possible return of the U.C.L.A. graduate to the scene of her college days.

It was apparent that a Tokyo Rose trial would be in accord with public sentiment, or at least in accord with such public sentiment as had been publicly expressed.

R.B. Shipley, chief of the passport division of the Department of State, then advised the Los Angeles city council that Tokyo Rose would not be allowed to come home.

"Give me five days in Tokyo," Brundidge told the FBI, "and I'll get the signature."

And so, on March 11 of '48, it finally happened that Brundidge and special agent John B. Hogan of the FBI boarded a plane for Honolulu and Tokyo. Brundidge was carrying four men's suits made of wool in his luggage. Wool was still scarce in Japan.

At Honolulu, he dropped by Clark Lee's place to pick up the penciled note from Iva Toguri to Clark Lee, signed "Tokyo Rose".

As Harry Brundidge's plane took off from Honolulu International Airport, Showman Earl Carrol (already in Japan) had finalized other plans for Tokyo Rose. He was going to make a musical comedy out of her. And, as it happened, due to an old friendship with General Douglas MacArthur, Carroll had the inside track to Iva Toguri over Brundidge and Winchell.

CHAPTER XI

TOKYO ROSE AS SHOW BIZ

In the early 1920's a showman named Earl Carroll was producing his famous 'Vanities' with a big floral wreath (in a horseshoe shape) above the stage door. As all of America knew at the time, the sign read: "Through these portals pass the most beautiful girls in the world".

A young officer from West Point also had permission to pass through and had done so whenever he could get a pass into New York. Since then, he had become far advanced in rank. In fact, he was General Douglas MacArthur. He always had been welcomed in Earl Carroll's penthouse, just off Times Square, and the General had never forgotten. That is why Earl Carroll was billeted at the American Embassy in Tokyo and given *carte blanche* to arrange for a documentary film on occupied Japan.

One of the prominent parts that Earl Carroll had in mind for the film was a dramatic treatment of Tokyo Rose. His plan was to cast Shirley Yamaguchi in a separate dramatic production about Tokyo Rose – a musical.

So, it happened that Iva d'Aquino was summoned to meet Earl Carroll on the same day, March 26, that she was also summoned to meet Harry Brundidge at the Dai Ichi Building, General MacArthur's headquarters building, across from the Imperial Palace, in Tokyo.

Iva was not feeling so well – she had lost the only child that she ever would have some ten weeks before. The child was stillborn.

Iva had no fear of meeting with Brundidge. She was confident that any subsequent investigations would result in her release, just as the Eighth Army investigations had. Her problem had been the same, now, for seven years – how to get back home. She ignored persistent evidence of shoddy treatment of Japanese Americans back in the States.

Faced with puzzling and complex motives of others, Iva chose not to attend the meeting with Brundidge – she turned back to her own simplifications.

Up to that time, Iva had never bothered to trace Brundidge's role in her troubles. She had never read Clark Lee's news notes, and didn't know of Brundidge's attempt to publish an article branding her as a traitor.

March 26th was a nice day at the Dai Ichi Building, and Earl Carroll was refreshing to be around. The people about him became beautiful, the future exciting. "I never met an ugly woman," he once told a New York reporter. "I never met a woman who couldn't be beautiful."

The day was full of cameras. Caroll took pictures of himself and Iva and a colonel, aide-de-camp to MacArthur. He took motion pictures in the yard of the United Press House of Iva with Shirley Yamaguchi. Then, at lunch, he took pictures of Iva, UP's Peter Kalisher and another newsman named Hobrecht.

The follow-up meeting with Brundidge was more like a command performance. Iva was brusquely escorted there by a sergeant from G-2 headquarters. Brundidge acted very official, and introduced her to a second man, Mr. Hogan.

"Mr. Hogan," Brundidge whispered to her, "is the man who signed your release in 1946." [1]

Mr. Hogan stood with his back to them, and took no part in the early part of the conversation.

"I am working with Mr. Hogan on your case," said Brundidge in the same guarded tone, "acting as an agent of the attorney general's office. Today may decide whether you will be able to go home, back to the U.S., or have to live in Japan forever." [2]

Hogan stepped back from the window and handed a briefcase to Brundidge, then turned back to carry on a conversation with a receptionist. From the briefcase, Brundidge pulled out a photostatic copy of a story written on Tokyo Rose. It looked to Iva like Clark Lee's story of 3,000 words or so from the 1945 interview. She handed it back to Brundidge, after scanning it.

"That's not the story I gave to Clark Lee," she said. "Most of it is made up."

Hogan turned and told Brundidge to get the other story. Brundidge then offered her a second document, saying "You remember the interview . . . Doesn't that look familiar?"

Iva hesitated, and Hogan prompted Brundidge, "Ask her if those are the notes of the interview."

Having never read the notes before, and immediately noticing some errors, Eva (now frightened by Hogan's manner, afraid her chances for going back to the States were dwindling with that man's displeasure) continued to hesitate.

Brundidge leaned over and said, again in his confidential tone, "All it will take to clear your way back to the States is your signature on this document."

Iva, her hope suddenly bolstered, signed the last page, "Iva Toguri d'Aquino", and under "witness" were entered the signatures, "John P. Hogan" and "Harry T. Brundidge", with the date of March 26, 1948.

Hogan, speaking to her directly for the first time, produced some "Zero Hour" scripts on onionskin paper, and asked her to identify and sign them. She did as requested. Then they went to Radio Tokyo, and she pointed out where the scripts were broadcast. After that, they parted company.

"How incredibly stupid it seems now – that meeting with Brundidge," recalls Iva. "I had no lawyer with me. But I really had nothing to hide. I wasn't worried about it."

Earl Carroll left that night for Hawaii, thoroughly briefed about the role of Walter Winchell in Iva's troubles, but unaware of Harry Brundidge's existence, and what he was up to.

Brundidge stayed on in Tokyo. He had other business to do.

With Iva's signed "confession" securely tucked into the briefcase, Brundidge selected a candidate for the eye witness to Tokyo Rose's treason. He was an old acquaintance, a Japanese travel bureau employee named Hiromu Yagi. Yagi accepted with enthusiasm. It was the best offer he had ever had – travel, warm clothing, and $10.00 per diem for an indefinite time.

Brundidge's prospect for a second witness was a friend of Yagi's, Toshikatsu Kodaira, who worked at UP in Tokyo. Yagi recalled the following story:

"One day during the war, in October or November of '44, Yagi was walking down the street near Radio Tokyo. There, he met a friend, and his friend told him of a propagandist who broadcast over Tokyo Radio.

"How interesting," thought Yagi, and asked his friend if he might see this propagandist in the act of broadcasting. Yagi's friend then led him into Radio Tokyo to the room where Iva d'Aquino made her broadcasts. There, in the monitoring room, Yagi saw and heard Iva and a Japanese boy in the act of broadcasting.

"With that story in mind, Yagi called Tosh Kodaira, and yelled into the phone, "Hey, Tosh, how would you like a free trip to the States?" [3]

"That sounded fine, said Tosh Kodaira. So, he met with Yagi and Brundidge outside of the Dai Ichi Building at ten o'clock the next morning to find out the details. Brundidge took them to his room and poured whiskey for all.

"Mr. Kodaira," Tosh remembered Brundidge saying, "Mr. Yagi here tells me that you both heard Tokyo Rose broadcast shortly after the March bombings in 1945 – that you both heard her say, 'Soldiers and sailors, your wives and sweethearts are enjoying themselves at home with war workers who are making big wages while you are fighting in the Jungles'. Is that true? Did you hear her say that?" [4]

"At that point, Kodaira recalled, he nearly dropped his glass of whiskey.

"Wait a minute," he said, "that never happened."

"Well, why don't you talk it over with Yagi," Kodaira remembered Brundidge saying, "and come back tomorrow morning."

"Then, Kodaira recalled, Brundidge walked to a closet and handed Tosh one of the suits of woolen clothing, and also picked up the half-full bottle of whiskey for Tosh to take along with him.

"The next morning, Tosh Kodaira handed an exchange gift to Brundidge, thanked him for the suit and whiskey, but said that he could not truthfully share in Yagi's story before an American jury, because it was a lie. Brundidge ignored Tosh from that time one, but told Yagi he had better get the story straightened out – perhaps with another friend.

"Tosh Kodaira said that he and Yagi then retired to a teahouse where he gave Yagi hell. Yagi said he was sorry. "Brundidge fooled me," said Yagi, according to Kodaira, "I'm not going to the States, either."

"The trousers and the vest that Tosh Kodaira had acquired from that incident were labeled "Harry T. Brundidge". Tosh took the suit to the U.S. Consulate in Tokyo, and had pictures taken of the suit there."

Back in California, from his world-famous restaurant on Sunset Boulevard, Earl Carroll enclosed a brief letter which he had received from Walter Winchell and sent it to Iva in Tokyo. In the letter, Winchell wrote of "a fair and open trial" for Iva. Carroll was mystified by that, and wrote, "I had understood that your trial days were over. I can't understand what Winchell means by 'a fair and open trial'." [5]

He would have a talk with Winchell, added Carroll, when he flew to New York in June, and try to call him off his "howlings" about Tokyo Rose.

Eleven days later, something representing the body of Earl Carroll was memorialized at Forest Lawn Cemetery, between two life-size floral chorines, consisting of 12,500 assorted flowers and a large, circular floral wreath with white on blue words enclosing a floral likeness of brunette Beryl Wallace and spelling out, "Through these portals pass the most beautiful girls in the world."

So . . . the man who might have turned the whole Tokyo Rose mess into a musical comedy review – as he had turned a 1936 bankruptcy in New York into a smash hit in Hollywood – was gone. He had been killed in a plane crash en route to New York.

Iva was now dependent upon the hard sell of Harry Brundidge to get her back to the States. She didn't know it yet, but Brundidge had already served notice of a different kind of homecoming that he had in mind for her.

CHAPTER XII

A BY-LINE FOR BRUNDIDGE

After almost three years, Brundidge's sensational news scoop on Tokyo Rose was finally published – not in *Cosmopolitan*, not in any magazine, but in a newspaper, the *Nashville Tennessean*. It was big news for the newspaper. It was bylined by "Harry T. Brundidge". It was copyrighted. And it covered the entire front page of the Sunday, May 2nd edition (1948), with more on the inside pages.

Brundidge was featured as crime buster and investigator. His picture was placed immediately under the banner headline. Also pictured were Iva d'Aquino, U.S. Attorney General Tom Clark (this was home country for him), and Special Agent John B. Hogan of the FBI.

Columnist Drew Pearson, Brundidge said in his story, tipped off the nation in a broadcast on April 11th that "Tokyo Rose has now given a full confession". Attorney General Tom Clark, the story went on to say, was contemplating her arrest. [1]

In a continuation on May 5th in the *Tennessean*, Brundidge was shown seated with a young Filipino who was identified in the cutline as "Tokyo Rose's Disc Jockey . . . now at Vanderbilt University". It was the ex-prisoner of war at Radio Tokyo, Norman Reyes. He and his wife, one of the early Tokyo Roses, Katherine Muraoka, were living in Nashville on student visas. Reyes, the story said, was expected to be called upon as a witness against Tokyo Rose.

Meanwhile, in Tokyo, rumors of such a trial had been current since Brundidge's visit in March. Practically everyone who had ever worked at wartime Radio Tokyo had been contacted, if not by Brundidge and Hogan, by FBI Agent Frederick G. Tillman or Provost Marshall James Wood. To the prospective witnesses – there were many of them – the chance to be sent to San Francisco as a witness at a Tokyo Rose trial had the nature of a social relief program. Times were terrible in Japan, and practically everything was scarce. The prospect of a fee ocean voyage and $10.00 per day expenses (soon to be raised to $12.00) looked like a fortune from all but the very highest paid job positions in Tokyo.

Iva had been warned repeatedly that she was in danger from false witnesses. Ruth Hayakawa paid her frequent visits to warn her about

Nakamoto, Mitsushio, and Oki. [2] The two Zero Hour supervisors, Ruth said, tried to get her to remember that she had heard Iva broadcast about a loss of ships following the Battle of Leyte Gulf in the fall of '44. A supposed offer of help came from stocky George Kazumaro (Buddy) Uno. [3] Uno said he knew the source of radio broadcasts about unfaithful wives and sweethearts, about jungle rot, and American GIs wasting away in the South Pacific (which was, of course, Myrtle from Radio Manila).

Among all of the people involved in the Tokyo Rose case, only two seemed strangely unmoved as the U.S. Government's belated search for witnesses gained momentum through the summer of '48 in Tokyo. One was former Lt. Colonel Tseneishi, the former boss of Radio Tokyo, and now a tea merchant, who realized, from the Tokyo Rose case, how little he had understood about Americans. Americans were a strange people indeed, he concluded, who busied their Justice Department with an inconsequential woman (one of their own), while he and his superiors remained uncharged.

When the investigations had begun in 1945, Tsuneishi had suspected some sort of ruse by the Americans to draw him off guard, but he knew now that the woman, Toguri, under the nickname of Tokyo Rose, was actually their central concern. That struck him as extraordinary, but if the Americans wished to make great matters out of such trifles, that was their business. He remained detached.

The other person strangely unmoved was Iva. She was like a person in shock. Perhaps it was the shock of her beloved America turning against her – or her disbelief that such a thing could actually be happening. Or perhaps it was, at least partly, the effect of having lost her child after carrying it for the full period of pregnancy. [4] Both physically and mentally, the pregnancy had been demanding. Then, the child was stillborn. In her circumstances it had been very disheartening.

Regardless, she was almost indifferent to offers of help. She was unwilling to take on the financial burden of hiring a lawyer.

Her marginal existence between two worlds had gone on for too long. She was trapped between massive forces which had sent her reeling back and forth for seven years.

"I am living a life of doubt," she told an Associated Press editor in Tokyo. *"I want my case settled once and for all."*

CHAPTER XIII

WHO WILL PROSECUTE TOKYO ROSE?

Inside the Justice Department, a Tokyo Rose treason trial was hard to justify. Not only had the Los Angeles District Attorney, James M. Carter, recommended against it. So had the U.S. District Attorney in San Francisco, Frank J. Hennessy.

To get a third opinion, U.S. Attorney General Tom Clark referred the case to special prosecutor, Thomas E. DeWolfe, the department's expert in matters of treason. DeWolfe had headed the government's recent wartime treason case against Chandler and Best in Boston, in which both defendants were convicted.

After investigating the evidence against Iva Toguri, DeWolfe also recommended against trying her for treason. In a remarkable memorandum to Raymond Pl Whearty, First Assistant U.S. Attorney General, DeWolfe spelled out why. The memorandum is dated May 25, 1948 – three weeks after Harry Brundidge had sensationalized the news in the *Nashville Tennessean* that a Tokyo Rose treason trial would be held.

The memo remained confidential in the Justice Department files until 1975.

Because of its importance in light of subsequent events, the memo is quoted here in full, just as Tom DeWolfe wrote it on May 25, 1948, shortly before the indictment of Iva Toguri as a treasonous Tokyo Rose.

*Office Memorandum*** UNITED STATES GOVERNMENT*

To: Raymond Pl Whearty   Date: May 25, 1948
From: Tom DeWolfe   TED'LA
Subject: Iva Toguri   146-28-1941

STATEMENT OF THE CASE

Reference is made to the above-entitled prospective treason prosecution, presently pending in the Department. Subject is not under restraint or in custody, and no criminal proceedings have ever been instituted against her in the United States.

Subject will be 32 years of age on 4 July next. She is Nisei, having been born in California of Japanese non-United States-citizen parentage. She graduated from the University of California, Los Angeles Branch, in 1940.

Her aunt was ill in Tokyo and subject's mother, being of unsound health, requested subject in the summer of 1941 to proceed to the Orient for the purpose of nursing subject's aunt. In July, 1941, lacking a passport but provided with a certificate of identification, subject sailed from southern California to the Orient. Having made the voyage without a passport and wishing to secure one, she visited the American Embassy in Tokyo and executed the appropriate application. *In the latter part of November 1941, she wished to return to the United States. She again visited the American Embassy for the purpose of obtaining a passport and was advised by American Embassy officials that they had received no authorization from Washington to issue her a passport.* However, the Embassy furnished her with a letter at that time stating that an application had been made for the passport. With this letter an attempt was made by subject to book passage on a ship scheduled to sail for the United States on 2 December 1941. She then learned that a permit was necessary from the Japanese Finance Ministry authorizing and empowering her to take out of Japan the money she had brought with her there from the United States. Before this permit was obtainable the ship had sailed and subject was left in Japan at the beginning of the war on 8 December 1941.

Finding it difficult to adjust herself among the citizenry of Tokyo through her *inability to speak the Japanese language, subject enrolled in the School of Japanese Language and Culture* in Tokyo shortly after her arrival and continued to attend this school until December, 1942. Early in 1942 she was advised that the passage would cost approximately $400 and that it would be necessary for her to pay the cost of the passage either before she left Japan or for someone in the United States to guarantee payment on her arrival in this country. Furthermore, she was told by the Swiss Legation that because of the fact that she was without a passport there was little chance that she would be evacuated to America on the first repatriation ship. In September 1942 she again went to the Swiss Legation in an endeavor to secure passage to New York on the Gripsholm but was unable to raise the amount of money required for the passage. After this occurrence she registered at a Japanese ward police as an alien and continuously thereafter until the fall of Japan was under the surveillance and scrutiny of the Japanese police.

With her funds becoming exhausted in July 1942 she obtained employment with the Japanese Domei News Agency as a typist in the monitoring section. In August 1943 subject obtained a part-time position as a typist at Radio Tokyo until November 1943. In November 1943, at the instigation of one Major Charles Cousens, an Australian prisoner of war, subject was selected through the medium of a voice test to participate as an announcer on Radio Tokyo's program called Zero Hour. She worked in this capacity approximately five days a week until 13 August 1945.

Three prisoners of war, to wit, Lieutenant Norman Reyes (Filipino), Major Wallace E. Ince (American), Major Charles Cousens (Australian), were in charge of the production of Radio Tokyo's Zero Hour broadcasting activities for the Japanese Government. *These three men have all been cleared by their respective governments of any charge of treasonous activity in connection with their alleged broadcasting work.* They will be the three most important witnesses against the subject if an indictment should be returned against her by a grand jury in a United States court. They will testify that subject broadcast no information of military or intelligence value and at no time beamed anything to troops in the southwest Pacific of a propagandistic nature. Her sole work, according to these witnesses, consisted of introducing musical recordings which were beamed to Allied troops in the southwest Pacific. They will testify that *they selected subject as an announcer because she was the only woman available, white or Nisei, whom they could trust not to betray to the Japanese their efforts to sabotage any propaganda* which the Japanese might and would attempt to broadcast to American troops when fighting in the Asiatic Theater. The three men above mentioned will testify that subject was likewise selected by them because she possessed a masculine voice which it was thought would not be attractive to Allied soldiers and fighting men in the Pacific. They will testify that subject never worked at the radio station more than two hours a day in the afternoon for five days a week in connection with her preparation for and actual broadcasting of the introductions to the musical recordings aforesaid. In order to earn a living to sustain herself subject was forced at the conclusion of her 20-minute portion of the program in question to work at the Danish Legation in Tokyo. The witnesses above mentioned will likewise testify that subject on some occasions made every endeavor to see that propagandistic matter was not inserted in or utilized by the Zero Hour program. *She frequently expressed pro-American sentiments in the presence of many witnesses and often evinced the wish and desire, when Japanese officials were not present, that the war would end soon, and that the United States, her native land, would emerge victorious therefrom.*

The three prisoners of war above mentioned who were instrumental in carrying out the program know as the Zero Hour and others will testify that subject aided American prisoners of war and often brought them food and sustenance. *The three prisoners of war above mentioned were, during a major portion of their broadcasting activity, housed in a rather luxurious Japanese hotel and were not under any more police surveillance than subject. They seem just as much, or more, culpable than she. The scripts of her programs seem totally innocuous* and might be said to have little, if any, entertainment value. The scripts containing the introductions to musical recordings, which scripts subject read over the air, were for the most part written for her in their entirety by Major Cousens (Australian prisoner of war).

The evidence at hand discloses that the appellation "Tokyo Rose" was never used by subject but was one indiscriminately given to subject or any one of five female announcers working at Radio Tokyo.

THERE IS INSUFFICIENT EVIDENCE TO MAKE OUT
A PRIMA FACIE CASE.

If an indictment is returned against subject by Federal grand venire men in the appropriate Federal judicial district the three Allied prisoners of war, Major Charles Cousens (Australian), Major Wallace E. Ince (American), and Lieutenant Norman Reyes (Filipino), will be necessary and material witnesses for and on behalf of the United States against subject at the trial on the merits before a petit jury. These witnesses have all been cleared of any charge of treasonable activity in connection with their work for Radio Tokyo. According to the available facts they were under no more duress or compulsion than was subject. As Government witnesses the Government will as a matter of law be forced to vouch for the truth of their testimony. They will testify to facts which will disclose as a part of the Government's case in chief that defendant lacked the requisite intent to betray. *It must be proved that the accused acted with an intention and purpose to betray or there is no treason. Cramer v. United States, 325 U.S. 1, 32.*

Here, anticipating the interposition of a motion for judgement of acquittal and assuming the verity of the testimony of the Government witnesses and all reasonable inferences that may be drawn therefrom, still *the Government's case must fail as a matter of law because the testimony of the Government will disclose that subject did not adhere to the enemy or possess the requisite disloyal state of mind.* Cramer v. United States, 325 U.S. 1, 30. If the situation were such that witnesses were available to testify that defendant actually broadcast propaganda to American troops in an endeavor to lower their morale and hinder and impede the American war effort and the defense produced evidence to combat said Government testimony, then a jury question would be presented but that is not the situation here.

The Government witnesses, almost to a man, will testify to facts which show that subject was pro-American, wished to return to the United States and tried to do so prior to Pearl Harbor, attempted unsuccessfully to return to the United States in 1942, and *beamed to American troops only the introduction to innocuous musical recordings.* The Government's evidence likewise will show that *subject was a trusted and selected agent of the Allied prisoners of war, who selected her as* the *one they could trust not to sabotage their efforts against the success of the Japanese propaganda machine.* In other words, the testimony which the Government will offer will not make out a case sufficient as a matter of law to withstand a motion for an instructed verdict.

It is also believed that the two overt acts against subject which are presently available i.e. proof from Reyes and Ince, prisoners of war, that subject broadcast two scripts in March 1944, are from a factual and trial standpoint insufficient as a matter of law. The two overt acts adverted to refer to broadcasts by subject which are nothing but introductions to musical recordings. There is no proof available that when subject committed said acts she intended to betray the United States by means of said acts. Cramer v. United States, 325 U.S. 1, 31. Such proof is a vital element of the Government's case before submission of the same to a trial jury is warranted. *The available proof on the overt acts committed by subject, i.e. broadcasting of two introductions to musical recordings in 1944, will not from a trial standpoint show that said acts were acts in furtherance of the Japanese war effort.* In the treason trials recently successfully concluded in Boston, Federal Judge Ford held as a matter of law that in order for an overt act to be sufficient to warrant submission of the same to the jury the proof thereon must show that the same was actually committed for the purpose of furthering the enemy's war effort.

There is no available evidence upon which a reasonable mind might fairly conclude guilt beyond a reasonable doubt and consequently a *motion for a judgment of acquittal under* F.P. Crim. P. 29(a) *would probably be granted by the trial court.* Curley v. United States, 160 F. (2d) 229, cert. den. 67S. Ct. 1511.

The statement of defendant given to Bureau Agent Tillman might not be admissible in evidence due to the fact that *subject was in military custody at the time and had been for some time without any military or civil charges ever being brought against her.* United States v. Bayer, 331, U.S. 532. Similar statements given to Department of Justice lawyers under similar circumstances were ruled out in recent trials in the Federal Judicial District of Massachusetts, although their admissibility was strenuously urged by the Government. *The proof available on the merits in the treason cases successfully concluded during the past year in Boston showed that the defendants in those cases expressed pro-German and anti-American sentiments,* broadcast propaganda from Berlin over the German Radio, *intended to dissuade American citizenry from supporting the American war effort,* and broadcast military information and information concerning the maritime losses of the Allied merchant marine, all obviously calculated and intended to impede and hamper the American war effort and lower the morale of American citizens. *The type and quantum of the proof available in the case against subject is the direct antithesis of that available and utilized in the Boston litigation aforesaid.*

The so-called "confession" or "admission against interest" given by subject to newspaper men Lee and Brundidge was given only after those gentlemen offered subject $2,000 for exclusive rights for subject's story, which was to be given to the Cosmopolitan Magazine, which journalistic enterprise said newspaper men represented. Of course, Lee and Brundidge at the time were not acting under the authorization of the Department of Justice but were acting in their private capacity. Any inducements held out by a private person who is not occupying a position of authority to secure a confession do not per se render the same inadmissible. United States v. Stone, 8 Fed. 232, Steiner v. United States, 134 F (2d) 931 (C.C.A.5), cert. den. 319 U.S. 774, 87L. Ed, 1721. However, the methods by which these newspaper men obtained the so-called "admission against interest" of "confession" from subject appear at least questionable and of doubtful propriety and would, no doubt, be submitted to the trial jury by the court for the purpose of enabling the petit venire men to determine whether or not the same was voluntarily obtained and was given by the defendant of her own free will.

RECOMMENDATION

Should the Department disagree with the views herein expressed and desire the case against subject to be presented to a Federal grand jury it is recommended that a no true bill be sought. Should an indictment be returned against subject under the applicable provisions of Title 18 U.S.C. Sec. 1 (treason) and the cause pushed for trial on its merit before a petit jury it is recommended that every possible effort be made to secure Federal Communications Commission records of monitoring of subject's broadcasts, which were until recently in the possession of the Federal Bureau of Investigation, together with the Naval sound track film and also the Naval Government recordings made of subject's voice in Guam, which matters are frequently mentioned in the numerous reports of the Bureau, which will be found scattered throughout the various sections of the file in this case.

In spite of DeWolfe's recommendation, U.S. Attorney General Tom Clark announced on August 16, 1948, that Iva Toguri d'Aquino would be tried for treason in the Twelfth Federal District Court in San Francisco. Thomas E. DeWolfe was assigned as the Special Prosecutor.

CHAPTER XIV

HOMECOMING

The troop ship, *USS General Hodges*, sailed majestically under the Golden Gate Bridge on September 25th, less than six weeks before the 1948 presidential election. On board were 2,000 men and Tokyo Rose.

The men on the upper decks went wild. Fire boats were out in full force. The city looked beautiful. It was a perfect day for a homecoming.

"By this time I was caught in an avalanche," Iva recalled. *"I tried to ride the waves as best I could – if you fight in deep water you're going to drown.*

"In the commissioner's office (U.S. Commissioner Francis St. James Fox), I saw my father for the first time in seven years. I didn't have a penny to my name. I came in without passport, papers, or identification one; they asked me where I was born and on what date, and that was it. I was in. Re-entry. I had tried hard enough and I got back, but it wasn't a method I would recommend to anybody else."

Her father embraced her and said, "I'm proud of you. You didn't change your stripes."

It had been seven years and 82 days since Jun Toguri had seen his beloved daughter. For him, also, it had been a rough seven years.

Early in 1942, he and his wife, Fumi, had been "relocated". Stripped of house and possessions, they had been moved, first to an abandoned race track at Tulare, California. There, Fumi Toguri had suffered a fatal stroke.

From Tulare, Jun Toguri was sent to a place of barbed wire, sharp winds, and even greater desolation – in Arizona. There, finally released at the age of 62, he had given up hope of resuming the life and business which it had taken him forty years to build in Southern California. He had gone to Chicago and started anew at an age when most men were looking forward to retirement. He had not known whether Iva was alive or dead until Clark Lee's story on her as Tokyo Rose had broken over INS in September of '45.

In San Francisco, Jun Toguri had received a cold reception all around, not only from Caucasians. The Nisei were not friendly either. They knew no more about the truth of the case than the Caucasians did.

For Iva a bitter realization sank in.

During her years in Japan, the truth about Executive Order 9066 (the presidential order of February 19, 1942) was inconceivable to her. Told of that order repeatedly by the Kempei tai agents in Tokyo, she had dismissed it as a pack of lies – just 'propaganda'.

Now, for the first time, she was afraid. She was shaken. These staring people with the blank eyes were not seeing 'her'. To them, she was just another Oriental. She sat numbly as the U.S. Commissioner read in stiff tones the formal complaint against her, cited two occasions, charged her with an undetermined number of acts "against the peace and dignity of the United States". She felt cut off – naked – vulnerable.

Stoic was the word for Iva Toguri, now – her own word. *"Stoic was an appropriate word for me . . . I was kind of numb. You know, you get dull – like a fighter gets punch drunk. The same situation goes on so long."*

Where were the Nisei? Why didn't they help? Why didn't they start a defense fund? Didn't they care?

In that post-war year of 1948, most Nisei, just out of relocation camps, were trying to get back to schools, find jobs, find places to live. Also, they were very aware of the fact that their own loyalty was still under question. And, most important of all, they were getting their information about Iva Toguri from the same sources the rest of America was getting it from – from the American press and radio, from Walter Winchell and Drew Pearson, and the U.S. Department of Justice.

Tamotsu Murayama could have told them . . . Tomotsu Murayama, who had been trapped in Japan much as Iva had been . . . he was an Associated Press correspondent quartered at the Sanno Hotel in Tokyo and forced to write radio scripts against the United States.

"We were all afraid of jeopardizing our positions, or possibilities of a position with the U.S. Occupation Forces. If we had had the courage to tell the truth, we could have squelched the whole thing in 30 minutes." [1]

The circumstances which had given such significance to her retention of U.S. citizenship, and had caused her to aid the prisoners of war, were now remote and obscure.

Matrons maintained a 24-hour suicide watch. Bobby pins were removed. Safety pins were taken away.

"How stupid," Iva sighed. *"If I wanted to die, I could do it by just giving up."*

But she did not want to die. On the contrary, the idea that, after all of these precautions, the U.S. Government might put her to death – that possibility dismayed her. It did not seem so remote a notion as it once was. Charges of treason, no matter how preposterously arranged, may bring the death penalty! The preposterousness of the charges had not seemed to deter them so far.

"Was she the loyal fool," she thought, *"the one who didn't 'catch the sign', who insisted upon playing by patriotic rules which all of those around her had so easily discarded?"*

Perhaps, in her situation, she had to simplify, or go mad.

She chose to simplify. *"The truth will come out,"* she believed fervently, *"The truth could not possible stay buried. The trial would free her at last."*

That night found her in San Francisco County Jail No. 3, where the matrons duly kept their 24-hour suicide watch over her. It was not needed. She slept like a baby – mingled with the fear and weariness had emerged a strong sense of resolve – and at last she was home. She was back in her beloved California. As the song says, "right back where I started from."

CHAPTER XV

INDICTMENT

With the approach of the Grand Jury hearing on October 6, San Francisco newspapers assigned federal court reporters to the case. They were an able and experienced group; Stanton Delaphane for the San Francisco *Chronicle*, Francis O'Gara for the San Francisco *Examiner*, Bill Burkhardt of the *Call-Bulletin*, Phil Hanley of the *News*, Katherine Pinkham, the Associated Press; Connie Hitchcock, International News Service; Hack Hanley, United Press; Paine Knickerbocker of the Oakland *Tribune*; Michi Onuma, San Francisco *Daily Mainichi*; and Marian Tajiri of the AJA Western States newspaper, *Pacific Citizen*.

Most of the prosecution witnesses who appeared before the Twelfth Federal District Grand Jury served double purposes – they could also be viewed as defense witnesses.

The government had problems. The grand jurors on the first day of hearings threatened to throw the case out. O'Gara got the story:

"A Government attempt to indict Iva Toguri d'Aquino halted yesterday over a reported disagreement between prosecution attorneys and members of a federal grand jury.

"In an unusual move, the jury insisted on the removal of all witnesses and federal prosecutors while they conferred among themselves.

"Later they recalled U.S. Attorney Frank J. Hennessy and his aides to the hearing room. The attorneys left twenty minutes later and announced the hearing would be postponed until tomorrow morning.

"While all such jury hearings are secret, members of the body said they were dissatisfied with the way the Government was running the case.

"One member said flatly that the attempted indictment of the American-born Mrs. d'Aquino was 'unfair' in view of federal failure to seek indictment against 'others just as responsible' for supposed treasonous wartime broadcasts." [1]

However, the proceedings ended with an indictment.

In the United States, treason is defined under Article Three of the United States Constitution, and requires the testimony of two witnesses to the same overt act, or a confession in open court, for conviction.

The statute which she would be tried under would be the United States Code at *18 U.S.C. § 238,* which states:

"Whoever, owing allegiance to the United States, levies war against them or adheres to their enemies, giving them aid or comfort within the U.S. or elsewhere, is guilty of treason and shall suffer death, or shall be imprisoned not less than five years and fined under this title but not less that $10,000; and shall be incapable of holding any office under the United States."

The key issue of the trial to follow would lie in paragraph three of the indictment:

That Iva Toguri d'Aquino,

". . being a citizen of the United States and a person owing allegiance to the United States . . . did knowingly, willfully, unlawfully, feloniously, intentionally, traitorously and treasonably adhere to the enemies of the United States . . ."

Indictment, Southern Division of the U.S. District Court, for the Northern District of California, No. 31712-R, UNITED STATES OF AMERICA, Plaintiff, vs. IVA IKUKO TOGURI D'AQUINO, Defendant

It was clear that everything, ultimately, would depend upon her intent. Without treasonable intent, the eight overt acts were innocuous. Without treasonable intent, there could be no treason under U.S. law, not even if one's action had caused the deaths of ten thousand countrymen.

The eight "overt and manifest acts" charged in the indictment were:

"1. That on a day between March 1, 1944, and May 1, 1944, the exact date being to the Grand Jurors unknown, said defendant, at Tokyo, Japan, in the offices of the Broadcasting Corporation of Japan, did discuss with another person the proposed participation of said defendant in a radio broadcasting program.

"2. That on a day between March 1, 1944, and June 1, 1944, the exact date being to the Grand Jurors unknown, said defendant, at Tokyo, Japan, in the offices of the Broadcasting Corporation of Japan, did discuss with employees of said corporation the nature and quality of a specific proposed radio broadcast.

"3 Said defendant . . (same dates, same outfit, same place) . . did speak into a microphone regarding the introduction of a program dealing with a motion picture involving war.

"4. That on a date between August 1, 1944, and December 1, 1944, the exact date being to the Grand Jurors unknown, said defendant, at Tokyo, Japan, did speak into a microphone in a studio of the Broadcasting Corporation of Japan referring to the enemies of Japan.

"5. That on a day during October, 1944, the exact date being to the Grand Jurors unknown, said defendant, at Tokyo, Japan, in broadcasting studio of the Broadcasting Corporation of Japan, did speak into a microphone concerning the loss of ships.

"6. That on a day during October, 1944 . said defendant . . did speak into a microphone concerning the loss of ships.

"7. That on May 23, 1945,. .said defendant . . did prepare a radio script for subsequent broadcasting.

"8. That on a day between May 1, 1945, and July 31, 1945 . . said defendant . . . did . . . engage in an entertainment dialogue" [2]

Upon receiving the indictment, Iva wrote a brief press release which was transferred on the AP and UP wire services, but received little play from news editors:

From Iva Toguri d'Aquino, Cell No. 3, S.F. County Jail:

"It was a grave disappointment to learn that the grand jury returned an indictment against me. It is my belief that if the Government attorneys had been interested they could have produced before the grand jury a number of material witnesses who could have cleared me of any suspicion of wrongdoing. The CIC and the FBI conducted a full and complete investigation into my life in Japan, and having found me innocent, they released me after I had been imprisoned for a year. I am innocent of any wrongdoing. I have faith in the court and jury and believe that they will be convinced of my innocence at the trial, and that I shall be acquitted of the charge brought against me." [3]

Among the working press, with few exceptions, Tokyo Rose was still entertainment – diversion from the important news of the day. That's what they had always used it for, and that's how they still used it. They sensed incongruity between their view of Tokyo Rose as entertainment and the much more serious Government view of her as a traitor.

Surprisingly, no one in the current media had traced the early war record of Tokyo Rose well enough to understand that "Tokyo Rose" was a legend, perhaps described even more accurately as a "myth", but there was a surplus of documentation to show that the U.S. Government prosecutors might as well have indicted the wind.

The special prosecutor, Tom DeWolfe, knew it. He wrote in a memorandum to First Assistant U.S. Attorney General Raymond Whearty, "It was necessary for me to practically make a fourth of July speech in order to obtain an indictment." [4]

And in a letter to Alexander M. Campbell, Assistant Attorney General, DeWolfe indicated that he wanted the Justice Department to undertake a second indictment against the American ex-war prisoner on Zero Hour, Wallace Elwell Ince.

> ". . I told the grand talisman that the case as to Colonel Ince, Mrs. d'Aquino's superior on Radio Tokyo, would be presented to a Federal grand jury here in the immediate future, after an exhaustive, factual investigation of the same in the Orient had been undertaken.
>
> "If the above action had not been taken by me, I believe that the grand jury would have returned a no true bill against Mrs. d'Aquino." [5]

So . . in order to justify the indictment of Iva Toguri in the minds of the grand jurors, DeWolfe had had to promise them a treason case against Ted Ince as well.

CHAPTER XVI

ROSES FOR THE DEFENSE

Times were terrible in Japan. The Tokyo Rose trial offered, in effect, a share in a half-million dollar economic opportunity program (the cost of the trial) for former Radio Tokyo employees and hangers-on. Although not all of the former announcers accepted.

The prosecution's list of 71 witnesses included 19 from Japan: eleven Japanese nationals and eight ex-American Nisei, including the former supervisors of Zero Hour, Nakamoto and Oki.

Said Wayne Collins, bitterly, "Every son of a bitch who ever set foot in Radio Tokyo was willing to testify against her for a free plane ride and $10.00 per diem. "Since the trial could take six to eight weeks to get going, and then, drag on for many weeks, the $10.00 per diem could amount to a lot of money."

President Harry S. Truman's favorite saying in the election campaign was, "If you can't stand the heat, stay out of the kitchen." In Federal Court circles in San Francisco, that translated to mean, "Don't be soft on traitors; if you have scruples about the Tokyo Rose trial, keep them to yourself".

So, flying first class to San Francisco came Hiromu Yagi, with eyes as bright as new pennies, to enjoy the $10 per diem at the Whitcomb Hotel while his scrupulous friend, Tosh Kodaira, grew thinner in Tokyo. And to San Francisco came Nakamoto and Oki to enjoy the good life at the expense of the U.S., and all for an hour or two before the grand jury and, perhaps, a couple of uncomfortable days under cross examination when the trial should get under way.

On they came, the militarists and the civilians – the executives, the clerks, the announcers, and the supervisors – all untouchable by the courts, all living well – all thanks to the stubbornness and adamant unwillingness of Iva Toguri to forego her American citizenship.

Notably missing from among the prosecution witnesses were the war-prisoners of Zero Hour and Bunka Camp. Norman Reyes, the only ex-PW who testified before the Grand Jury, had switched to the defense.

The lack of a defense fund hurt in many ways. The defense could offer neither passage fare, nor expense accounts, nor immunity from prosecution for defense witnesses from Japan and Australia.

Late in October, the prosecution released a news story that ex-PW Capt. Ted Ince (recently promoted from major to captain) would appear as a "star witness against the defendant". [1] DeWolfe was counting on the threat of a treason trial to intimidate Ince into testifying for the prosecution. But Ince remained steadfast for the defense – and hired his own lawyer.

On the first Tuesday in November – November 3, 1948 – the political goal of the Tokyo Rose trial was satisfied. Harry S. Truman won re-election over Thomas E. Dewey

"What would have happened," the only republican among the defense attorneys (Theodore Tamba) was asked, "if the republicans had won?'

"Most likely," he answered, "the trial would have been thrown out to save money. The democrats had every political hack in Washington in on the prosecution." [2]

Tamba was the man sent to Japan for the Defense on a budget of $3,000 at Government expense. He had the task of finding defense witnesses and documents in Japan – from the same sources which U.S. Army and Government prosecutors had been raking through for three years.

"I never saw so many scared people in my life," said Tamba. "The occupation forces had turned Japan into a brothel. Our tax money was being thrown in all directions while the Japanese were dependent upon the occupation forces for jobs."

Forty-three depositions were taken by Tamba before Vice Consul Thomas W. Ainsworth of the U.S. in the Mitsui Bank Building, with Attorney Noel Story representing the prosecution. Tamba could have used six months in Japan to good advantage. Instead, he petitioned for and got a delay of the trial's opening from May 16 to July 5.

Among the 43 witnesses were three potential Roses. One was Foumy (Fumi) Saisho (usually introduced as Madame Tojo), undoubtedly the first actual broadcaster at Radio Tokyo who was referred to as Tokyo Rose by listening GIs. Another was Lily Ghevenian, who used to type and occasionally announced the Zero Hour scripts at Radio Tokyo. The third was Ruth Hayakawa, the soft-voiced woman who had lent a highbrow touch to Tokyo Rose with her Sunday broadcasts of semi-classical music.

First, Tamba questioned the original Madame Tojo, Foumy Saisho. [3]

"Did you ever hear anybody mention the name 'Tokyo Rose' in conversation with you?"

"There was mention of Tokyo Rose toward the end of the war."

"Did you ever have a conversation with Ken Oki about Tokyo Rose?"

"Yes."

"What was the conversation?"

"I asked him if Tokyo Rose indicated any particular person. He said that it did not represent any particular person, but it was used in broadcasting to the American soldiers."

"Did you ever have a conversation with Mr. Oki to the effect that he thought he was entitled to one-half of the royalties for the use of 'Tokyo Rose'?"

"Yes."

"Was that in reference to the use of the name 'Tokyo Rose'?"

"Yes."

Beyond the brief "yes and no" answers, Foumy Saisho was noncommittal.

The Armenian-Japanese Rose, Lily Ghevenian (also known as Lily Sagaoyan) [3] recalled that Iva Toguri once had broadcast something over the air about being Tokyo Rose, and that led to her testimony about the motives of Ken Oki and George Nakamoto.

Attorney Noel Story asked the first set of questions.

"Do you recall making a statement to Mr. Tillman (FBI Agent Frederick G. Tillman) . . and I quote: 'Miss Toguri talked to me about being referred to as 'Tokyo Rose' and was happy about it and was all smiles'. Did you sign that statement?"

"No, I did not."

"Do you recall telling Mr. Tillman that?"

"No, I do not."

"Did you ever tell Mr. Tillman that Miss Toguri mentioned being 'Tokyo Rose' over the air?"

"I remember one time she said such a thing."

"That she made such a statement over the air?"

"As far as I remember, she did."

After the cross examination was completed on that deposition, Tamba took up the same line of questioning on redirect examination:

"Were any other girls referred to as 'Tokyo Rose'?"

"In the radio station?"

"Yes . . ?"

"They did not know who Tokyo Rose was."

"Were any of the other girls suspected of being Tokyo Rose?"

"Yes."

"Who were they?"

"Ruth Hayakawa and June Suyama."

"Any others?"

"That's all I remember."

"In answer to one of Mr. Story's questions, you said you heard Miss Toguri broadcast over the air that she was 'Tokyo Rose'?"

"She did mention it; it was in the script."

"Do you know whose script that might have been?"

"No."

"Who brought you that script?"

"I do not remember whether it was Ken Oki or Iva."

"It could have been Ken Oki who brought that script?"

"Yes."

"But you don't recall who actually broadcast that remark?"

"I do not."

". . . You have asked other people why they were testifying against Iva when she did nothing wrong?"

"Yes, I have talked to them."

"And what did they tell you, in substance?"

"These people who testify against her, they told me to go ahead and have a good time and get a free ride to the United States like they did."

"Will you tell us who these people are, if you remember?"

"Ken Oki did."

"Anyone else?"

"Other people who went on that trial won't even say hello to me."

"They are trying to avoid you?"

"That's right."

"Who is trying to avoid you?"

"Nakamoto (George Mitsushio)."

"Anyone else, if you know?"

"No."

Ruth Hayakawa remembered, in her testimony on deposition, the first day she had heard the name, Tokyo Rose, and the ensuing conversation she had with assistant Zero Hour supervisor, Ken Oki, about it. On direct examination, Tamba asked if she had heard the name Tokyo Rose, and she answered:

"Yes, I first heard the name 'Tokyo Rose' in 1944, when Ken Oki asked me whether I had read the newspapers of that day. I recall definitely that it was Sunday evening, and when I told Ken Oki that I had not seen the papers, he showed me a copy of news that came in from the Foreign Office, which said the GIs in the south were enjoying the radio programs from Tokyo, especially the music and the voice of a young lady, and this article said that the woman's voice was very soft and appealing, and they liked the program, and they wondered who 'Tokyo Rose' was; so, I recall asking Ken who was 'Tokyo Rose' and Ken told me that it was I, because the article said Sunday evening, and I was on the Sunday evening program, and also Ken pointed out that my voice was soft and appealing, whereas Iva's voice was not." [4]

The flesh-and-blood Roses who actually had broadcast over Radio Tokyo were now one fewer in number, Tamba learned. June Suyama had been killed in an auto accident in 1947, in Tokyo.

Meanwhile, back in the States, the prosecution was having more troubles as the trial date neared. Harry Brundidge's attempt to bribe Tosh Kodaira had become known, and Clark Lee was infuriated. The special agent who had accompanied Brundidge to Japan, John B. Hogan, wrote a memorandum dated May 26, 1948, to the Justice Department files (addressed simply to "The Files") which told of a warning from Brundidge that Lee had written six UPI articles denouncing the Government trial of Iva Toguri, and may be sympathetic to the defense:

"This afternoon, Harry T. Brundidge telephoned me from New York and advised that the information he was about to give me he had received in confidence, but felt that the government should have it.

"Clark Lee prepared and submitted to International News Service for publication a series of six articles. The title and the general subject matter of these articles were unknown to Mr. Brundidge. He stated that among other things the series included a most bitter and vitriolic denunciation of the Government for having considered a prosecution of the defendant in this case. The language of the article was so bitter against the Government that Mr. Barry Ferris, Editor and Chief of INS, returned it to Lee, refusing to have anything to do with his publication. It was Mr. Ferris who gave this information to Mr. Brundidge. The conclusion which Mr. Brundidge draws from the above facts is that Lee will most likely be extremely sympathetic to the defendant if called to the stand by the Government." [5]

Alexander M. Campbell, Assistant Attorney General, Criminal Division, sent the following memorandum to Attorney General Tom Clark, dated June 8, 1948:

*Office Memorandum ** UNITED STATES GOVERNMENT*

To: The Attorney General   Date: June 8, 1949

From: Alexander M. Campbell   AMC: JBH: mmv

Assistant Attorney General, Criminal Division   146-28-1941

Subject: *United States v. Iva Toguri D'Aquino—Treason*

You will recall that by memorandum dated December 2, 1948, we informed you that, then prospective Government trial witness, *Yagi, had given a statement to the Counterintelligence Corps in Japan to the effect that his testimony before the Grand Jury in San Francisco was false* and that *he had given his testimony,* as well as his previous statement, *to an attorney of the Criminal Division at the suggestion and urging of witness Harry Brundidge.* You will also recall that *witness Brundidge when confronted with this statement simply denied it in total.*

We are now in receipt of a *statement by Yagi made in Japan to an FBI agent reiterating his accusation in somewhat greater detail.* We also have a statement from another Japanese, *Toshikatsu Kodaira,* which states that in effect that he, Kodaira, *was also requested and urged by Brundidge and Yagi to give a similar false statement.*

The *defendant's attorney,* who was in Japan obtaining depositions for and on behalf of the defendant, *is aware of the recent revelations made by Yagi and Kodaira, and will cross examine Brundidge* in the regard when and if he takes the stand as a Government witness at the trial on the merits herein. The testimony expected of Brundidge at the trial of this case will be corroborated by evidence from other credible sources.

The trial of the instant case is scheduled to begin at San Francisco on July 5, 1949.

In considering the possibility of instituting prosecution against Brundidge for subornation of perjury, we believe that such action taken prior to the completion of the litigation involving Iva Toguri D'Aquino would completely destroy any chance of a conviction in her case. We further believe that it would be *unwise to initiate such prosecution of Brundidge at any time* because *the chance of convicting a white man upon testimony of two Japanese, particularly in California, is very slight.* We also feel that the fairly close friendship which existed between witnesses Yagi and the newspaper man Brundidge for a considerable number of years would probably result in Yag's refusal to testify against Brundidge on grounds of self-incrimination.

In view of the foregoing, *it is strongly recommended that at the present juncture no federal criminal proceedings of any sort be initiated against Harry Brundidge* for any alleged Federal statutory offense arising out of the facts hereinbefore discussed. This Division is likewise firmly of the view that there is no reasonable expectation from a factual standpoint of a successful ensuing Federal criminal prosecution subsequently against Brundidge based on the facts which are the subject matter of this memorandum.

(Italics—the author's)

DeWolfe already had decided not to call Hirom Yagi to the witness stand because of his complicity in the attempt to bribe Tosh Kodaira. Now, DeWolfe also scratched from the list of prosecution witnesses the name Harry T. Brundidge.

CHAPTER XVII

TRIAL

Trial day – July 5th, 1949 – exactly eight years since Iva Toguri embarked for Japan.

The San Francisco courtroom was a relic of budget surplus . . . a dumping ground for a million dollars which had to be spent by the end of the fiscal close in the year of the earthquake, 1906, or go back to the federal treasury.

Under an incredibly high ceiling, the floor space was crowded. Stretching to that ceiling were rounded columns of roseate marble, topped by plump cupids of justice which hovered in stone, staring blankly at the marble white floor. The witness seat rose to prominence beside the judge's bench.

Defense and prosecution tables were within whispering distance of each other, flanked by the raised jury box on the left and the press table at right, as one faced the judge. Spectators were crammed into 110 seats, beginning just inside the massive, gilded doors. Mounted above all that, 72-year-old Michael J. Roche sat in flowing black robes before the stone mosaic. It was rumored that Judge Roche was so grateful to be appointed court justice by the FDR administration that he had danced a delighted jig in the marble hallway, fourteen years before.

Had Iva Toguri been the flamboyant and seductive Tokyo Rose which most thought her to be, perhaps more like Myrtle Lipton of Radio Manila, she would probably have taken advantage of that rococo setting, forcing her accusers to drag her into the courtroom, clad in revealing rags, shedding tears of innocence like Paulette Goddard casting as a street waif in a Chaplin movie. That Tokyo Rose would have had every male aching to aid and comfort her.

But diminutive Iva strode into the courtroom without one touch of ornament, hurriedly and independently, with her left arm held lightly by Bailiff Herbert Cole, clad in an aged tan, glen plaid suit, with out-of-date lines and padded shoulders, like a member of some obscure military auxiliary, her hair drawn severely into an inverted V in the front with a bun on the side. Contrary to what most of the courtroom audience had expected, she was strictly a plain-Jane, dressed in the usual conservative manner to which she was long accustomed.

"I wasn't a clothes-horse defendant," said Iva in a masterpiece of understatement. *"It wasn't my nature to be flippant about it or jovial or be appealing or work toward sympathy . . . it was a stiff, cold courtroom, and I thought everything was going to be judged in a stiff, cold manner."*

She couldn't have been more wrong. Behind his scholarly manner, dome-browed Tom de Wolfe was prepared to cover her like a billboard with a gaudy, home-front image of the treasonous Tokyo Rose.

But DeWolfe was not happy with the role that he was about to play. Bill Burkhart of the San Francisco *Call-Bulletin* shared an inside tip he had gotten from Federal court employees, with Katherine Pinkham, the federal court reporter for the Associated Press, that DeWolfe was not enthusiastic about prosecuting the Tokyo Rose case.

"I think he took it on,' said Burkhart, "as a career obligation. He's a life-long Democrat, a pro. They told him to take it, and he had to take it."

Later, Katherine Pinkham wrote, "Of my own knowledge, I can attest that at least one of the Government prosecutors had no stomach for this job. I believe there were two. U.S. Attorney Frank Hennessy, whom I had know for many years, told me in confidence that he had recommended against prosecution after looking into the case and reviewing the transcript of the Army hearing, at the request of the U.S. Attorney General, Tom Clark. Mr. Hennessy's recommendation was overruled in Washington and a special prosecutor assigned to his case. I was told later by those close to him (DeWolfe) that he, too, was not happy in his role."

Happy or not, DeWolfe was preparing for an all-out effort. In his rooms in San Francisco's exclusive Canterbury Apartments, one could see his work lights burning into the morning hours. He rarely went out – and tended to go alone, when he did.

DeWolfe had a thankless task in which the facts were being revealed more and more obviously not to fit the Government's buildup for the trial. Compared to the landmark cases of treason in American history, the matters set forth in the Tokyo Rose indictment were petty stuff, indeed. This case lacked magnitude and any sense of a serious wrong having been committed.

As a matter of American history, there had been only two Americans convicted of treason prior to World War II. The earliest had been Thomas Wilson Dorr, a Rhode Island political reformer and advocate for equal rights. In an effort to rectify the inequities in voting rights, he and a small number of supporters led an attack on the Rhode Island state arsenal on May 17, 1842. Three weeks later nearly 2,500 government troops stormed the rebel fortifications on Acote's Hill in Chepachet. Dorr escaped to Connecticut, but a Grand Jury indicted him for treason in his absence, and sentenced him to life imprisonment. When Dorr finally returned to Rhode Island in October, 1843, he was immediately arrested and imprisoned. Due to ill health, however, Dorr only served one year, and an Act of General Amnesty released him on June 27, 1845.

The second successful treason trial was against John Brown, an anti-slavery activist and a voluntary agent for the "underground railroad", which shuttled escaped slaves from the U.S. south to Canada. In 1859 John Brown led a party of 21 men to over-run the Federal armory at Harper's Ferry, hoping that his action would encourage slaves to join his rebellion. The armory was retaken by a company of marines under Robert E. Lee two days later. John Brown was tried and convicted of insurrection, treason, and murder, and was executed on December 2, 1859.

Much has been written to try to explain the post-WWII mood that prevailed in America. Patriotism ran high, and there were still strong feelings against the Germans and the Japanese, even a touch of racism. The democratic Truman administration was being challenged as being "soft", which included its prosecution of WWII traitors, and 1948 was re-election year. Some have suggested that the deployment of the atom bomb at Hiroshima and Nagasaki had injected a certain psychological twist, a paranoia. Mingled with all of this was also an emerging fear of communism, later to express itself with the McCarthyism "Red Scare".

This same prevailing mood that had pressed for Iva Toguri's indictment also prompted the conviction of seven others for treason during the post-war years (1947-52). Four of these were for radio broadcasts for the Axis powers in Europe: Douglas Chandler, Martin Monti Robert Best, and Mildred Gillars. Another trial was against Hans Max Haupt, who was convicted of treason and sentenced to life in prison (March, 1947) for aiding his son, a German spy. The seventh was Tomoya Kawkita, an American citizen, found guilty of torturing American prisoners of war while working as an interpreter for the mining company, Oeyama Nickel, during WWII in Japan. He was finally sentenced to death in 1952.

Douglas Chandler was the first found guilty of "treason by radio". Introduced over the air at Radio Berlin as "Paul Revere", he was bitterly anti-Semitic and anti-American, and was fined $10,000 and sentenced to life imprisonment (August, 1947).

Martin James Monti, then a second lieutenant in the USAAF, defected to Germany in October, 1944, taking his P-38 Lightning aircraft with him. He introduced himself as "Martin Wiethaupt" on German radio, broadcasting anti-American propaganda. After surrendering to the Americans in '46, he was initially charged with desertion, and pardoned on condition that he join the U.S. Army. The FBI rearrested him in 1948, charged him with treason, and he was sentenced to 25 years in prison.

Robert Best was another found guilty of "treason by radio", and was sentenced to life imprisonment (March, '48) for his propaganda broadcasts from Radio Berlin as "Mr. Guess-who".

Mildred Gillars, whose nickname among the Allied troops was "Axis Sally", had introduced herself as "Midge at the mike" in her broadcasts with Radio Berlin. Gillars was originally charged with 10 counts of treason, later reduced to eight. The prosecution had argued that Gillars had signed an oath of allegiance to Nazi Germany, and had posed as a Red Cross worker in order to record messages from American soldiers that could be used in her propaganda broadcasts. After a sensational six-week trial, the jury convicted Mildred Gillars on only one count of treason, on March 8, 1949, just four months prior to Iva Toguri's trial date. Gillars was sentenced to 10 - 30 years.

It is worthy to note that the World War II trials for "treason by radio" wrote a new chapter in the law of treason in the United States – these convictions were for actions which provided no significant aid or comfort to an enemy, and were not committed within the territorial jurisdiction of the U.S.

Now, came this incredible trial of Tokyo Rose.

Selection of an all-white jury took only a couple of hours on this first day of trial. Six black Americans and one Chinese-American were excused on peremptory challenges by the prosecution. Six of the jurors selected were classified as housewives (Babette Wurts, Fannie Ibbotson,

Adele Grassens, Edith Schlobohm, Glora Covell, and Mrs. Ival Long). Two were paint firm employees (not the same firm), Robert Oakes and Robin E. Stevenson. One, Robert L. Stout, was retired. The remaining three included a plasterer, Earl M. Duckett; a bookkeeper, Matthew J. Yerbic; and a Certified Public Accountant, John Mann. The sole alternate was Mrs. Aileen McNamara, a housewife, also white.

On the morning of the second day, DeWolfe took the floor for his opening address. The courtroom was packed and quiet. He built slowly into an oration. The deliberate manner maintained was in contrast to the emotionally charged appeal he was making to the jury.

"We will show," DeWolfe told the jurors, "that in one broadcast after the Battle of Leyte Gulf, she told American troops: "Now, you boys really have lost all your ships. You really are orphans now. How do you think you will ever get home?

"We will show that she told American troops that their wives and sweethearts were unfaithful, that they were out with shipyard workers with wallets bulging with money; that she told them to lay down their arms, that the Japanese would never give up and had the will to win. And that there was no reason for Americans to stay there and be killed.

"We will show that she would pick out a favorite spot familiar in the United States – like Los Angeles – and say, "How would you like to be back in Los Angeles tonight, dancing at the Coconut Grove with your best girl? How would you like to be parked with her in Griffith Park listening to the radio?"

"We will show that she talked about the mosquitoes and the jungles, and when she heard some troops were short of food, she told them they should go home where they could get steak and french-fried potatoes; that, once, when she heard a certain unit was short of water, she broadcast: 'Hello, sarge, got any beer down there? Forget about the beer. Wouldn't you like some cold water? Cold water sure tastes good'." [1]

The first witness called by the prosecution (the first of 71) was a jaunty young man, J. Richard Eisenhart, ex-Eighth Army guard at Yokohama Prison, who presented to the jury's gaze a one-yen note with the signature, "Tokyo Rose", on it, and pointed out the defendant as the one who signed her name to it.

This was clearly an emotional distortion by the prosecution. If the trial was to be cast upon an emotional bias from the early Pacific war legend, then Orphan Ann was already distorted – out of focus, removed from any possibility of objective judgment – she was already obscured beneath the stereotyped image of the early legend of Tokyo Rose.

In the first two trial days of press coverage, Iva Toguri d'Aquino was described by the trial reporters as "passive", "silent and impassive", "Japanese by race", "undistinguished", "dressed without ornament", "the petite, Los Angeles-born Japanese defendant", and one who sat "quietly in a position directly facing the flag", and as one who "gave no outward sign of interest". Furthermore, the press was allowed no access to her outside of the courtroom. In the limited view that the press was expressing, hardly anyone could have identified with the defendant, even if they had tried. The prosecution view was dominant in the press.

CHAPTER XVIII

TSUNEISHI

At the end of the first week of trial, the first important witness, the straight-backed, thin-lipped former military boss of Radio Tokyo, Tsuneishi, took the stand for the prosecution. Artist Howard Brodie of the *Chronicle*, chose the moment to capture the essence of the courtroom scene in a sketch.

Tsuneishi sat with legs crossed, arrogant, "tough, unconquered, and unreconstructed" (as Delaplane described him), with interpreter David Swift beside him. All eyes of the jury and the spectators were on Tsuneishi. In his view of the defense and prosecution tables, Brodie caught the lawyers in a swirl of activity over and about the defendant, who was further obscured in her loose-fitting suit.

"I always had a feeling that I was irrelevant to the trial," said Iva long afterward, and Brodie had caught that feeling about her in his sketch in the *Chronicle* (July 17, '49)

One did not often see a Japanese warrior like Tsuneishi as captive witness. At Tarawa, Kwajalein, Saipan, Americans saw such men only in death – their bodies torn by whatever weapons were at hand: in the absence of a ceremonial dagger, a gun; in the absence of a gun, a grenade – sometimes blown into disfiguration with a comrade, face to face.

The Samurai doctrine never involved Harakiri without meaning. To men like Tsuneishi, the act was not purely voluntary. It was prescribed for certain conditions and situations. Defeat had not occurred in any climactic struggle for the homeland in which one could assemble the troops for that last dramatic ceremonial act. Instead, a technological development, a new bomb, had ruled Harakiri irrelevant to the national defeat.

Tsuneishi, due to the circumstances of the Japanese defeat – the stunning power of the A-bombs at Hiroshima and Nagasaki – was alive and on the witness stand in San Francisco.

"Given the circumstance," he said at one point in the questioning, "I am here."

The words were almost the same ones that he used on the witness stand to explain why the PWs had broadcast over Radio Tokyo. They did so, he said, "because of the circumstances of that time."

In the San Francisco *Chronicle* of July 7th, appeared a picture of Tsuneishi, looking at a 1942 issue of *Life Magazine*. The widely-set eyes gazed at the joyous celebration by the troops of Lt. Gen. Masaharu Homma (since executed by the United States for war crimes) during their triumph over the Americans at Corregidor.

If the U.S. Government's priorities as to whom to try for war crimes was different, Tsuneishi might have suffered the same fate as Homma, or that he was on trial, not Iva Toguri. His policy of forcing PWs to broadcast, and the documented stories of threats and beatings that could be mustered against him would score heavily against him. The irony of his position escaped the court and the public – except, that is, for the ex-war prisoners of Bunka Camp. They remembered him when . . . !

But here, he was involved in the trial of a clerk-secretary, whose broadcasting assignment had been of so little import in his mind that he had not remembered her, except as one of the dozen faces which he had seen infrequently as he had passed the typing pool. For Tsuneishi, the world pictured in the 1942 edition of *Life* was the real world, and the San Francisco world of the Tokyo Rose trial was a surreal curiosity.

"I was in charge of broadcasting to weaken the morale of the enemy," Tsuneishi testified under direct examination by DeWolfe. "I was in charge of Zero Hour, which was used to make Allied troops homesick and tired or disgusted with the war."

The PWs were not forced to broadcast, he affirmed. "There was absolutely no threatening or violent language used in having them do so."

The prisoners were driven in limousines without guards, back and forth from Bunka Camp to the broadcasting studios, said Tsuneishi. They wore civilian clothes, were allowed a great deal of freedom. There were no threats, was no force of any kind.

The direct examination was brief. Tsuneishi was under cross examination before the noon recess on Monday, July 12.

From the depositions gathered by Ted Tamba in Japan, Wayne Collins had quite a different picture of Tsuneishi's operations with the war prisoners than he had been hearing from the witness stand.

Katsuji Mori, vice chief of the Overseas Broadcast Planning Office at Radio Tokyo, had testified on deposition as to the incident in which Tsuneishi had drawn a sword, lain it across the desk, and confronted Cousens with an official Japanese Army order to broadcast or get his head cut off.

"What would have happened to Major Cousens if he had refused to obey this order?" [1] Tamba had asked Mori in the deposition.

"I don't know exactly what would have happened to him," Mori had replied, "but it was an order. So, I guess something would have happened to him."

Yuman Ishihara, a translator at Radio Tokyo, had testified that he, also, was present in Tsuneishi's office when the Army order was read to Cousens, commanding the Australian to broadcast. The entire chain of command which led to the order was recalled in a deposition by Katsutaro Kamiya, chief of the English Language unit at Radio Tokyo.

Further evidence of threat and coercion was in the deposition by Tamotsu Murayama, the former Associated Press newsman; Tsuneishi had the Bunka Camp PWs lined up before him and told them, "You are ordered to cooperate with the Japanese Army to broadcast. If you fail to cooperate, your life is not guaranteed", [2] so Murayama recalled.

Of course, none of the depositions had been submitted into evidence and wouldn't be until the defense case was offered, but Collins could guide his questioning by them.

The cross examination of Tsuneishi started quietly. It was slow going. Collins asked the questions in English, which were then translated into Japanese to Tsuneishi by the interpreter, David Swift. Then, Tsuneishi answered in Japanese, which was translated into English for Collins. (It was a wonderful way for a witness to gain time to think about his answers.)

By Tuesday afternoon, July 13, Tsuneishi was opening up to Collins about the defendant and the other Roses of Radio Tokyo.

He couldn't remember any specific quotations by Iva Toguri as Orphan Ann, said Tsuneishi. He didn't understand English, and he had never spoken to the defendant individually. He had not assigned her to the Zero Hour, he recalled. He hadn't ordered Nakamoto to include any woman on Zero Hour. He recognized thirteen other English-speaking women who had broadcast from Radio Tokyo to Allied troops in the Pacific: Mary Ishii, Ruth Hayakawa, Foumy Saisho, June Suyama, Kay Fujiwara, Mieko Furuya, Margaret Kato, Katherine Muraoka, Yoneko (Ruth) Matsunaga, "Mother" Fayvelle Topping, Dr. Lillie Abegg, Fusai Sakaebara, and Frances Tompkins.

Now, Tsuneishi was beginning to sound like a witness for the defense. The Zero Hour never got beyond the point of short wave entertainment, in order to build up listener interest among American troops, he said, because the war ended abruptly, and he had been saving his Sunday punch on that program for an all-out defense of the Japanese mainland – something that never happened.

Collins pressed the point, "You have stated, Colonel, that the purpose of the Zero Hour was to endeavor to undermine the morale of the U.S. and Allied troops . . . that was the purpose of the Japanese Army, wasn't it?"

"It was," Tsuneishi answered.

"And you know," continued Collins, "that the purpose was actually defeated, wasn't it, by the persons conducting the Zero Hour?"

"I did not think the broadcasts were poor," the witness responded.

"They were ineffective, weren't they?"

"In my opinion," Tsuneishi used his words carefully now, "the lowering of the morale of the enemy was not entirely carried out, because of the earlier conclusion of the war, but – as you know, the basis of propaganda is to appeal to the enemy. Viewed from that angle, I can consider that it was a success."

Tsuneishi did not understand the Zero Hour when he heard it in English, he said, but he was given a Japanese translation of the Zero Hour scripts from which the musical sections had been omitted. (According to Cousens, that was why he had such great leeway to mix the messages on the program when Nakamoto's failure to provide home front news or commentary enabled Cousens to fill with impromptu musical interludes.)

Then, the questioning got tougher. The topic shifted to conditions under which the defendant and the PWs had broadcast at Radio Tokyo, and the witness clammed up.

". . . You told Lt. Reyes and Capt. Ince that they would obey orders the same way that Major Cousens was compelled to obey your orders."

"I do not believe I told them to obey my orders."

"You told them to obey the orders of Mr. Mitsushio and Mr. Kamiya, isn't that true?"

"Yes, but in my opinion those were not orders, but the instructions of directions of those gentlemen . . . "

"And Mr. Mitsushio was accepting the orders of the Japanese Imperial Army Headquarters, isn't that true?"

"As regards the internal workings of the broadcasting, I gave directions to Mr. Mitsushio."

"Mr. Mitsushio carried your orders into execution didn't he?"

DeWolfe saw a duress argument forming for the defendant and threw a barrage of objections, most of which were sustained.

Collins protested, and read Tsuneishi's order which he had delivered to the assembled War Prisoners at Bunka Camp in "an offer of proof", designed to get it into the trial record over the prosecution's sustained objections.

Tsuneishi's version was very different. He recalled, "in a general way," that he had said to the PWs one fall day in '43:

"Unfortunately for both of us, war has developed between Japan and the United States. You people, unfortunately, have acquired the position of prisoners of war. We believe it was not necessary for Japan and America to have gone to war. A war is a matter of extreme loss to both sides. It is my desire and wish, therefore, that this war be terminated as soon as possible. If you will cooperate with my wishes and ideas, you will broadcast to the American people that this unfortunate war be terminated as soon as possible. If there is anyone present who does not wish to do this, please step forward." [3]

"Who stepped forward?" asked Collins.

"A Britisher, George Williams, a person who came from the Gilbert Islands," answered Tsuneishi. "A splendid type of Britisher."

The court allowed no further questions to Tsuneishi about the Bunka Camp incident. The defense protested.

"We desire to show," said Collins, "that there was continuing duress stretching from the day Major Charles Cousens was assigned to perform duties on the Zero Hour to the date that it was concluded; that it was part and parcel of the *res gestae* (facts of the case, admissible in evidence)."

But prosecution objections were sustained. Collins' questioning became tenacious. Tsuneishi acknowledged that a written order was read to Cousens when the Australian was "persuaded" to broadcast over Radio Tokyo for the first time. However, DeWolfe's objections were sustained to prevent the witness from answering as to what the order had meant or whether the presence of an unsheathed sword had been used to enforce it.

Collins turned to the bench once more.

Judge Roche recessed court. In the absence of the jury, DeWolfe for the prosecution and George Olshausen for the defense joined argument in a key struggle to decide whether or not duress may have relevance for the defendant in this trial. (Note that the condition of duress had already been used to exonerate the Bunka Camp PWs from military punishment for their wartime broadcasts.)   DeWolfe argued, "the interrogation this morning, the line of questioning to which your honor sustained my objection, did not address the defendant's intent. It went to alleged duress of others fifteen months prior to the time that subsequent proof will show they were associated with the defendant . . It did not deal with the defendant's intent in any manner whatsoever; so, with all due respect to Counselor Olshausen, I say he misconceives the requested instructions."

"I don't believe that I misconceive the point of the Government's instructions," responded Olshausen. "The Government's instructions are that the Government can prove matters not pleaded in the indictment in order to show guilty intent, and we say, for the same reason, we can prove matters not pleaded in the indictment to prove innocent intent . ."

"Duress on others," continued Olshausen, "so far as communicated to the defendant and so far as it is part of the duress on the defendant, is relevant to the question . . There is a chain of proof here, and we cannot put in all our proof with one witness or with one question . ."

"There is nothing before the Courts," ruled Judge Roche.

The effect of the ruling was that Tsuneishi never had to acknowledge or deny his threats to Cousens or the presence of his bared sword on the desk before Cousens as he was read an Imperial Japanese Army order to broadcast or else. The line had thus been drawn by the Court's ruling between oppressive conditions which had applied to the war prisoners at Radio Tokyo and those which might have been applied to the defendant.

The court ruling would have far reaching effects in the trial. It meant that the testimony on depositions by the war prisoners would not be allowed in the court record. The jury would never hear the vivid, detailed description about Tsuneishi's "persusion" methods used on the PWs, nor the food situation at Bunka, which was detailed in the deposition by Dutch Lt. Nicolas Schenk, the Bunka Camp cook: [4]

"We had a speech every day for two or three months," Schenk had testified, "intended to break us down mentally and to force us to believe that there was no way out – one line I particularly remember is that 'nothing is guaranteed'. Tsuneishi told us the wall, which we saw around us, could be climbed easily, but anyone who did it would come back in pieces."

"The daily diet for the PWs, said Schenk, consisted of "three tea cups of corian per day, a kind of corn . . . to fill the bellies of chickens, and its effects were severe beri beri and pellagra; and three bowls of soup to get that down with. The bowls were a little larger than the tea cups. The soup consisted of dikon, which is horseradish, a little salt, a little soya, to which water was added."

All of the PWs had malnutrition, said Schenk, and he named individuals and their ailments.

"McNaughton had boils. Major Cox was flat on his back for three months, not able to move. Larry Quilly lost 40 pounds in about six months. I suffered diminishing eyesight and, later, leg deterioration. All of us had beri beri. Kalbfleisch and Streeter also had temporary blindness. Larry Quilly lost his hair."

"Cousens and Ince," Schenk had continued to Tamba in the deposition, "brought some foodstuffs they got from Radio Tokyo. An old lady and her husband living in the basement of our quarters were sent once in a while to get us some food items, and we collected the young leaves from the trees, which had been proven edible in Singapore. I, personally, killed two cats. Frank Fujita killed another couple of cats, and we consumed them. We ate at least two dogs."

"The PWs were slapped around by Japanese officers, said Schenk. "Larry Quilly was beaten repeatedly. Ince was beaten severely. Henshaw was beaten, also Parkyns, Shattles, and myself. Lt. Hamamoto, a sergeant from the Kempei tai, Uno, another Japanese named Hishikara, and Endo beat us. Ikeda never beat PWs. Ince, weighing 130 pounds, was called out to do exercise by the Kempei sergeant. Ince had to bend his head low and that made him dizzy. He couldn't get up. Hanamoto ran out from his room into the courtyard directly up to Ince and knocked him out. Ince was unconscious for a few minutes. I know Hamamoto's swing . . pretty severe because he knocked me out, myself, when I complained about food, and it took me four days to recover from that."

At one point in the deposition Schenk had described Tsuneishi as "smart, sword rattling, and arrogant, with an inferiority complex before white men."

Schenk's deposition might have shown for Collins exactly how close the relationship was between Iva Toguri and the war prisoners. Schenk had spelled it out, when Noel Story had asked him, on cross examination in the deposition:

"Why are you so anxious to help someone who collaborated with the Japanese Government . .?"

In broken English, Schenk had replied:

". . . Treason to me is when a person does something for gain, to get something out of it for personal benefit or out of a belief – while I personally did not believe that anybody, a Nisei boy or a Nisei girl working in Radio Tokyo at that time, which the Japanese regarded as neither fish nor fowl, would be regarded as a traitor – to commit treason. .

"I would be willing to defend her only on the fact already that she helped the prisoner of war by giving information or anything else . . . I certainly feel this is a part of my duty to help that girl after what she had done, even if it had not been done to myself. During that time we regarded ourselves as so close together, we went through so many things, that it was no difference whether it was for me or any of us . ."

That kind of familial concern between the PWs and the defendant was exactly what Collins wanted to establish, and could have established if the defense had been given wide enough latitude to go into the context in which the defendant had given sustained aid to the war prisoners. That had justified the broadcasts made by the PWs and it could do the same for the defendant. DeWolfe's job, clearly, was to draw a distinct line between the prisoners and the defendant, and to keep it drawn.

CHAPTER XVIV

LEE

Clark Lee fretted and stewed in his Whitcomb Hotel room on Market Street. Tsuneishi's testimony would be concluded soon. Lee was next. Lee's friend, Stan Delaplane, dropped by with a bottle of whiskey. Lee drank and talked about the trial. Then, he took another drink and talked about something else, only to drift back to the trial.

"All I want to do is get up there and get it over with,' he said.

"Lee was a nervous as a cat," Delaplane said. "I think if he had known in 1945 what he knew in July, 1949, he would have written a different story. But by then, it was too late. Things had gone too far." [1]

Lee knew about the real matrix of Tokyo Rose – the early war rumors. He had first heard the name in January or February of '42 at Corregidor in the Philippines. Without linking Iva Toguri to the passage in his book, *One Last Look Around*, he had described the whimsical nature of Rose-type rumors:

> "The story that Radio Tokyo . . . knew every move made by the American Army is one of the most persistent of the war. It began shortly after Pearl Harbor, and as far back as April, 1942, when a group of us escaped from Bataan and reached Australia, we were told that Radio Tokyo had reported our arrival and had said, 'Glad you made it to Australia. We'll be down after you before long.' When a fighter squadron or a bomber group moved to a new base, dozens of people reported that Tokyo Rose had said, 'Hello, there, you boys of the Three Hundred and Nineteenth. Hope you'll enjoy the Philippines more than you did New Guinea.' Every new transfer was supposed to be announced by Tokyo Rose the day it was made. However, I never found anyone who had heard such broadcasts himself. It was always the guy in the next tent." [2]

On the morning that he was to testify, Lee had a bad throat. His voice sounded like fingernails on a blackboard. But he looked great. A flutter of excitement ran through the crowded courtroom as he took the witness stand. He was the first real celebrity among the witnesses – an internationally famous war correspondent with books to his credit. He was identified in court as a free-lance writer living at the Monterey Peninsula Country Club, Del Monte, California.

Despite defense objections, DeWolfe placed into the trial record Lee's news notes – the so-called "confession", as Exhibit 15, and a note attached to it with Iva's signature on it as Tokyo Rose (Exhibit 14). Two pages of the original 17 in Clark Lee's news notes were missing.

Over further vigorous defense objections, DeWolfe sought to link Lee's story with several of the eight overt acts of the indictment, particularly no. 6 – the one concerning the loss of ships.

Lee stated:

"She said that in the fall of '44, at the time that Japan claimed they had sunk a number of American ships off Formosa, a major came to her from Imperial Headquarters and bluntly suggested that she broadcast as follows: 'Orphans of the Pacific, you really are orphans now. How are you going to get home now that all of your ships are sunk?"

DeWolfe: "Was any statement made to you by her at that time as to American wives and sweehearts at home?"

Collins: "I object to that as leading and suggestive, deliberately prompting the witness."

Court: "The objection will be overruled. He may answer."

Collins: "It is not part of her statement."

Lee: "She said that she said in her broadcast that she told the truth, that their sweethearts were unfaithful to them, that their wives were out dancing with other men while they were fighting in the muck and jungle."

DeWolfe: "Was any statement made by her to you at that time, Mr. Lee, as to the reason she took this post, financial or otherwise?"

Lee: "Yes."

DeWolfe: "What did she say?"

Lee: "That she needed the additional hundred yen a month to live one."

DeWolfe: "Mr. Lee, you can answer the next question yes or no. Was any statement made by her at the time concerning the difficulties, if any, of her position?"

Lee: "Yes."

DeWolfe: "What did she say?"

Lee: "She said that compared to the other girls – to what the other girls had to do at the studio her work was rather easy, and she sometimes felt selfish about it, that all she had to do was face the mike and go home." [3]

After another thirty minutes of that, Collins moved to strike out the whole of Lee's testimony on the grounds that no foundation was laid for it. The motion was denied, and cross examination began. Collins probed into Lee's prior knowledge about the legendary nature of Tokyo Rose.

Collins: "When did you first hear that name, 'Tokyo Rose', if you can recall?"

Lee: "I think it was during the siege of Bataan at Corregidor."

Collins: "That was, Mr. Lee, in the year 1942, wasn't it?"

Lee: "Absolutely."

Collins: "Yes. So, that the person that you designated to Mr. Leslie Nakashima as 'Tokyo Rose' was the broadcaster for Radio Tokyo in the year 1942?"

Lee: "When you put it that positively, I am not sure. It may not have been until the Solomons, it may not have been until later on."

Collins: "You wish to change your testimony, Mr. Lee?"

DeWolfe: "I object to that as being argumentative and unfair."

Court: "Objection is sustained."

Lee: "I do not wish to change my testimony. You asked me when I thought it was. I said I thought it was then, but I did not say I was sure. It may have been six months later. It may have been when I read about it . ."

Collins: "Six months earlier?"

Lee: "Six months earlier there was no war, so it could not have been then."

Collins: "Bataan fell in April, 1942, didn't it, Mr. Lee?"

Lee: "Absolutely."

Collins: "So, if you heard it six months later, you still heard it in 1942?"

Lee: "If I did, yes, that is correct. I do not believe I ever heard a broadcast of Radio Tokyo except when we were going in on B-29 raids, which was in 1944."

Collins moved to the arrangement with Iva d'Aquino as Tokyo Rose at the Imperial Hotel interview.

Collins: "Mr. Lee, isn't it a fact that the very first thing she told you and Harry Brundidge and Leslie Nakashima at that time and place was that she was not the only girl on Radio Tokyo, and that she was not 'Tokyo Rose'?"

Lee: "That is not a fact. It is half true. She said she was not the only girl, but she was the 'Tokyo Rose'."

Collins: "Did you ask her if there were any other persons who were 'Tokyo Rose'?"

Lee: "No . . . It did come out in the course of our discussion that there were several girls, but who said it, I do not know."

Collins: "Isn't it a fact that you do not know which one said the defendant was Tokyo Rose? Isn't that a fact?"

Lee: "No, it is not. I know that she said it. It was the whole thing, the whole idea of the interview. We were not just looking for – that is not what we were looking for when we started out."

Collins: "You were looking for a story, weren't you, Mr. Lee?"

Lee: "Of course, we were looking for the story of Tokyo Rose, and our whole interview and conversation was based on the fact that Mrs. d'Aquino had identified herself as Tokyo Rose and signed a contract as Tokyo Rose. If she had said, 'I am not Tokyo Rose', that would have ended it."

Collins: "You offered her that contract, you and Mr. Brundidge, didn't you, if she would state that she was Tokyo Rose?"

Lee: "No, that is not put in exactly the right way. If she were Tokyo Rose, then we wanted her story. If she were not, then, of course we didn't want it."

Collins: "So then any female announcer from Radio Tokyo would have served your purpose, isn't that correct?"

Lee: "No, that is not correct. Unless that female had identified herself as Tokyo Rose and been able to make it stick."

Collins: "Mr. Lee, when the contract was offered to the defendant, you then were of the impression that you were getting a contract from Tokyo Rose, a female broadcaster, who had been broadcasting from Radio Tokyo from away back early in 1942, isn't that a fact?"

Lee: "That is partly correct."

Collins: "Yes?"

Lee: "It is not entirely so, though. I can't say that it goes all the way back to 1942; as I say, I don't remember when I first heard it, but we thought it was a broadcaster who had been on the air for a long time."

Collins: "Going back to some time in 1942?"

Lee: "Perhaps to 1942 – I can't say for sure when that name started, Mr. Collins. I do not know – they did start to listen to enemy radio from almost the beginning of hostilities, but when the female voice started, I do not know when it was." [4]

Lee knew that it was coming sooner or later, but he could not be sure when – the questions about the meeting between Brundidge, himself, and Collins – about Brundidge's trip to Japan. It didn't come that first day of cross examination.

The next morning, Lee's throat was rougher than ever. Collins seemed to be skipping from one topic to another. First, he was on the "Battle of Formosa" – a battle that never was. Then, Collins turned to other matters which had not appeared in Lee's notes. Then, Collins brought up a pre-trial meeting involving himself, Lee, and Brundidge.

Collins: "On October 25 of 1948, Mr. Lee, at the St. Francis Hotel in the presence of Mr. Brundidge and Mr. Edward Hoffman, you told me, didn't you, that you were one hundred percent for Rose?"

Lee: "I never made such a statement in my life."

Collins: "You never made any such statement?"

Lee: "No."

Lee apparently was not comfortable in the witness chair. He shifted back and forth. DeWolfe was listening more intently. He sensed something unusual going on.

Collins: "That meeting was held at your request and at Mr. Brundidge's request, wasn't it?"

Lee: "I think Brundidge phoned you. I don't believe I did."

Collins: "Well, you were willing to participate in the conversation we had, weren't you?"

Lee: "I certainly was, yes."

Collins rocked back on his heels and slammed the next question like a man delivering a blow.

Collins: "Now, Mr. Lee, isn't it a fact that you and Mr. Brundidge requested me to go to the St. Francis Hotel on October 25 of

1948 because you wished to ascertain from me at the time whether or not I knew that Harry Brundidge had gone to Japan in 1948 and while in Japan, advised Yagi to come before the Grand Jury and testify falsely in this case?" [5]

There it was – a bribery charge. DeWolfe was on his feet, shouting "objection" before the last words were out of Collins' mouth.

The objection was sustained – but the headline word, "bribery" would be on the front page of every newspaper in town the next day.

After court recessed for the day, Lee told Delaplane, "I wanted to answer him (Collins) on the stand, but DeWolfe wouldn't let me. I didn't know then or now what Brundidge did at the time in question." [6]

There was a basic irony at work in Lee's testimony. If Lee had been captured at Bataan or Corregidor, which he surely would have been had he not been taken aboard a U.S. submarine on February 22, 1942 (as part of General MacArthur's escaping entourage), and if he had survived his capture by the Japanese at that time, he inevitably would have been assigned to writing scripts along with the Associated Press captive, Tamotsu Muryama, and all of the other Allied newsmen captured by the Japanese. Under Tsuneishi's policies, Lee would have been in more or less the same position as Charles Cousens.

Under recross examination, Collins concentrated on the two "quotes" of Lee's which related directly to alleged overt acts no. 6 and no. 7. Collins read from Lee's notes "they'd bluntly suggest, you fellows all without ships. What are you going to do about getting home? Orphans of the Pacific, you really are orphans now".

"Now, these notes," said Collins, "or that note that I just read to you, as a matter of fact, is more accurate than the statement you made from the witness stand this morning, isn't that true?"

"Undoubtedly, yes," answered Lee.

"Now, Mr. Lee, turning to page 12 . . . fifth paragraph, it reads as follows:

"I imagine them sitting in jungles, swatting flies and mosquitoes, sweating under tropical sun. i play cooling music, semi-classical, music by eric coates, the Englishman; gershwin, soft vocals by maxine sullivan, lawrence tibbett. once in a while light operas or classics. vary to hit all sorts of listeners."

Collins paused to look at the witness, "She did make that statement to you, didn't she?"

Lee answered, "Yes, sir."

Collins: "And now, Mr. Lee, this morning, or rather yesterday, you state on cross examination . . 'She said that she said in her broadcasts that she told the truth, that their sweethearts were unfaithful to them, that their wives were out dancing with other men while they were fighting out in the muck and jungles.' Did you make that statement?"

Lee: "Yes."

Collins: "Now, Mr. Lee, no such statement as this appears in the whole lot of your notes of your interview with her September 1, 1945, at the Imperial Hotel in Tokyo."

Lee: "That is correct, Mr. Collins, but I can tell you the circumstances."

Court: "You wish to explain your answer, you may explain."

Lee: "When I finished typing these notes and I got up from the table to stretch, the defendant and Mr. Brundidge were over by the window and he was taking pencil notes and I walked over there and at that time she made that statement or one very similar to it. He wrote it down and I saw him write it down and I saw those notes again in 1946."

Collins: "Do you know where those notes that carried any such statement, made in the writing of Mr. Brundidge, are?"

Lee: "I don't know where they are. I think the FBI has them."

Collins: "Did you read them when it was written?"

Lee: "I saw it written and read it, and read it again when I was preparing notes."

Collins: "Haven't you talked to Harry Brundidge recently?"

Lee: "I saw him last Tuesday morning, briefly. I think I saw him Thursday morning for a few minutes."

Collins: "Now, Mr. Lee, as a matter of fact, May 5 of 1949, you came to my office in the Mills Tower Building in San Francisco; Mr. Olshausen was present. You were present and I was present. Don't you recall that?"

Lee: "Yes, sir."

Collins: "And didn't you state to me at that time that you could not testify to any conversations you had with 'Rose', that you had forgotten, that the only thing you could testify to would be from what your notes show?"

Lee: "No, I told you this morning I don't recall making any such statement."[7]

As Clark Lee quit the witness stand, followed by the admiring glances of just about everyone in the courtroom, he took with him a favorable impact for the prosecution case far in excess of any factual basis that he had in his testimony. The idea that Lee's news notes were a reliable record of what Iva Toguri had told him, that his interpretation of the notes was objective, that in a three hour interview, almost four years before, he had gotten to know the woman and her intentions – all of that was conjectural.

But, smitten by the war reputation of Lee, by the role of glamour correspondent which he carried off so well with a handsome and dashing presence (like Clark Gable at his best), not a juror in the courtroom was critical of anything that Lee had said. Neither was the defendant.

Said Iva d'Aquino, *"The second time I ever saw him was in court. Some of the papers say I glared at him when I met him on the way out of court. I don't think I glared at him. I don't think he was a bad person. Had circumstances been otherwise, I might have liked him."* [8]

Considering the damage that Lee's testimony had done to her, that was an amazing statement.

CHAPTER XX

THE "ZERO HOUR" WITNESSES

Tom DeWolfe had a problem. His problem was: How to make two disloyal American Nisei palatable as eye witnesses to the alleged treason of a third loyal American Nisei. George Mitsushio and Ken Oki, the two supervisors of Zero Hour, if not managed carefully on the witness stand, could repulse Judge Roche and flip his sympathies to the defendant.

DeWolfe got Mitsushio and Oki on and off the witness stand quickly. On direct examination, each testified in hushed monotones to seven of the eight overt acts of alleged treason – testified identically, using words right out of the indictment, culminating in a word-for-word quotation about what Iva Toguri had said over a microphone at Radio Tokyo almost five years before: "Now, you fellows have lost all your ships. You really are orphans of the Pacific. How do you think you will ever get home?" [1]

Judge Roche, moved to distaste for Mitsushio, allowed wide latitude for questioning in cross examination, and Wayne Collins heaped scorn and ridicule on the ex-Zero Hour boss.

"Can you repeat the oath of allegiance to the flag?" asked Collins of Mitsushio, knowing that the former San Francisco Nisei had been a Boy Scout and, then, an ROTC student at UC, Berkeley.

DeWolfe objected, but Judge Roche overruled the objection and Mitsushio had to answer. He swallowed hard. Sweat beaded his face. He appeared to be choking.

"I pledge allegiance . . . to the flag . . of the United States of America . . and to the republic for which it stands . . one nation . . indivisible . . ."

He stopped, then mumbled, "I don't remember."

Judge Roche completed the oath from the bench, ". . . with liberty and justice for all." [2]

Then, it was Oki's turn. Collins taunted Oki by pointing out that Oki didn't seem to recall anything about the happening of an unspecified day at Radio Tokyo in October, 1944, except the exact words which were broadcast by Iva Toguri.

"What did you have for breakfast?" said Collins. Oki shook his head.

"For dinner?" Collins persisted. "What time did you go to work? . . What did you wear?. . . Was the day cloudy?. . . Sunny?. . . Well, what was it?. . . Was it snowing?"

Oki could recall none of those things, but he remembered the exact words of the defendant about ships, just as Mitsushio had recalled, "Now, you fellows have lost all your ships. You really are orphans of the Pacific. How do you think you will ever get home?" [3]

"Where did you get those witnesses?" growled Judge Roche to Frank Hennessy, as Oki left the stand.

Hennessy hadn't gotten those witnesses. Brundidge had, but the jury and the general public never realized that the man named Harry T. Brundidge was connected with the actual Tokyo Rose trial, and Judge Roche would not be exposed to Brundidge, either.

DeWolfe had struck the name of Brundidge from his list of witnesses.

Following the testimony by Clark Lee, Brundidge had left town quietly. The defense never knew that Brundidge had been responsible for procuring Mitsushio and Oki as prosecution witnesses.

CHAPTER XXI

THE RECORD SHOW

At last, the jurors would have a chance to use the earphones which had been dangling beside them for the past four weeks of trial. Interest quickened. What, exactly, had Orphan Ann done and said over the Radio Tokyo microphones?

Five of the recordings had been made 7,500 miles from Radio Tokyo in Portland, Oregon, and the sixth had been recorded 10,000 from Tokyo in Silver Hill, Maryland. Only four programs were involved on the six records – those of August 11, 14, 16, and September 15, 1944.

None of the material on the six discs, explained DeWolfe to the jurors, related to any of the eight overt acts of alleged treason. He was submitting them merely as voice identification.

The first disc was spun. A needle was put to it, and George Gershwin's "Strike up the Band" sounded in the earphones. At the defense table, Iva laughed for the third time in the trial (she had laughed when Mitsushio had choked on the oath of allegiance and another when Tom DeWolfe, who did not move gracefully, had tripped and dropped the only disc with a complete program recorded on it). The voice of Orphan Ann crackled on top of the music.

Ann: "Hello, there, you fighting orphans somewhere in that pool of
water called the Pacific. This is your playmate, Orphan Ann,
taking roll call . ." [1]

The voice sounded barely intelligible. It crackled, faded, and occasionally washed out. The first two scripts were clearly innocuous.

But the jurors still were listening expectantly as script number three began.

Ann: "Hello, you fighting orphans in the Pacific. How's tricks? This is
after-her-weekend Annie back on the air strictly under union
hours. Reception OK? Well, it better be because this is all request
night."[2]

The jury was showing little interest. The defendant was taking notes. The fourth and final script was coming up.

Ann: "Hello, to the fighting orphans of the Pacific. This is of course your favorite playmate, Orphan Ann, with Friday's invitation to listen to good music . . . in other words . . . music for you. It's been so long since you boneheads have listened to one single orchestra in one single city . . . let alone dance to one. I'm getting you boys into condition . . . just in case, mind you. Never know when you'll be able to afford the price for a cover charge, flowers, and so forth. A nice orchestra is all set to entertain you."

MUSIC: (1) Strike up the Band, (2) My Mother Would Love You, (3) Day in, Day out, (4) Holy Smoke! Can't You Take a Joke?, (5) Do I Love You, Do I, and (6) Goodbye, Now. [3]

If the defense had called for dismissal of the charges immediately following the playing of those recordings, the press table, at least, would have been in favor of the motion.

Francis O'Gara described the total effect.

"Interest heightened, and it looked like the big moment was about to begin. Instead, 23 pages of recordings transcript produced just a dull thud – perhaps even duller than the recordings themselves, which were too indistinct for anyone to hear without earphones and amplifiers. It placed her behind the wartime microphones of Radio Tokyo, but that was about all."

Paine Knickerbocker of the Oakland *Tribune* projected another thought:

"It seems to me that the Government has so frail a case that it shows a basic weakness – no evidence exists. Obviously, if there had been damning evidence, it would have been preserved."

Thinking along those line, knowing that the Eighth Army CIC investigators and the FBI agents had access to all of the Orphan Ann recordings in the investigations of 1945-46 in Japan, why hadn't the recordings for October of '44 been saved? Where were the alleged "quotes" recalled by Lee and Mitsushio and Oki about sunken ships and 4Fs out with the sweethearts and wives of the GIs? It defied reason to think that such damning statements would have been discarded if Orphan Ann had made them. Nothing from the OWI file on Orphan Ann, recorded in the Pacific, had been saved? How terribly careless of someone – and convenient!

CHAPTER XXII

THE LETTER

From the three million or so friendly enemies of Orphan Ann – the wandering Orphan family of the Pacific – the prosecution had selected nine to proclaim her an enemy. They were carefully selected from hundreds who had responded to the Justice Department's ad for witnesses to broadcasts by Tokyo rose (first printed in the New York *Times*, December 4, 1947. And on one of them, DeWolfe had set a kind of booby trap for Wayne Collins.

Wayne Collins' style in cross examination of witnesses was predictable. As Phil Hanley described it in the San Francisco *News*, Collins "not only overturns all stones . . he also grinds them into sand. Then, he examines the grains one by one." [1]

On the morning that Marshall Hoot, ex-crew chief on a crash boat in the Gilbert Islands, was to testify, Hoot put into his pocket a five-year-old letter which he had written to his wife from Abemama, in the Gilberts, to his home at Alhambra, California.

Preceding Hoot to the witness stand, three ex-servicemen already had testified that they had heard Tokyo Rose, alias Orphan Ann, throwing verbal fire bombs, and in one case, ice cream sodas. [2]

On direct examination, Hoot recalled Tokyo Rose saying, "Congratulations, Commander Perry, on your safe landing, but you'll be sorry if you don't leave now." And they were sorry, said Hoot. "Any time she said anything was going to happen, it happened." [3]

On cross examination, Wayne Collins probed for the time of the broadcast, the call letters of the station involved, and frequencies. The time, said Hoot, that Commander Perry landed his plane at Abemama was 2:00 p.m. on December 29, 1943, and the broadcast came about two hours after that. "I remember," he said, "because I wrote this letter . ."

And out came the letter.

The letter said nothing about call letters, about frequencies, about Orphan Ann or about Zero Hour, but it told about a high and low-level bombing attack by Japanese planes, following a broadcast by Tokyo Rose. Two of Hoot's shipmates were killed, it said, and he helped bury them. "Please store up some liquor," the letter went on, and then concluded, "Honey babies, I hope I dream of you tonight as I think of you all day." [4]

The letter sent the six women jurors fumbling in their handbags for handkerchiefs. It hardened the jaws of the men. At the press table, said Delaplane, the odds for acquittal "broke like the 1929 stock market."

But the greatest damage to the defense was not immediately apparent, and did not become evident until almost a decade later. Three days before Christmas, in the year 1958, Katherine Pinkham and the author called on Judge Roche in his office at the Federal Court Building. The judge was a gracious host. His kindly, Irish face was ruddy and cheerful. His eyes were bright. He was 81, still active on the federal court bench – one month away from his retirement. He said slowly and earnestly, pausing at some length between phrases:

"The human race . . . is a study . . . It's human to err . . . I've always taken the simple path in life. I think . . . if it wasn't for the witness from Loss Angeles, the reluctant witness . . . I might have considered her innocent. They pressed him to tell and he produced that letter. I think, up to that point . . . that was the turning point. Up to the time that fellow pulled the letter out of his pocket . . . with all my experience . . . I was up in the air as to what might or might not . . . have happened." [5]

The judge was talking about Marshall Hoot.

The judge then turned aside to Katherine Pinkham, whom he had known for more than a score of years, and said to her, "You know, I always felt there was something peculiar about that girl's going to Japan when she did. I always thought she might have been up to something."

Clearly, the personal sign of truth, the authentic sign of Iva d'Aquino's guilt, for Judge Roche, had been the impassioned letter of Marshall Hoot to his wife.

CHAPTER XXIII

DURESS

"I was attracted to the scene by screams. It was night and there were lights . . and there were these naked Japanese, naked except for a Fundoshi, a G-string sort of affair, and they were beating a coolie . ."

Charles H. (Bill) Cousens, for almost four years war prisoner of the Japanese, was establishing the groundwork for a defense plea of duress. The scene was on the dock at Singapore in March of '42. As Cousens spoke, his voice lowered. His gaze became distant.

"The word got around amongst the boys – he was starving and had rushed in and had tried to snatch a can of food from a Japanese soldier . . . They threw him to the ground and put his head under a tap so that as he drew breath and screamed, he drew water into his lungs. And then they drew him away, and he got up and they proceeded to beat him again, and then they put him under the tap again, and so on . . .

"Eventually, they put him under the tap, and I suppose he clenched his teeth because they broke his face open on the tap, turned the water on, drowned him, and threw the body away." [1]

Prosecutors Tom DeWolfe and James Knapp were paying no attention to Cousens, thinking that Collins was still in the preliminary stages of setting background with his key witness.

"What did you see with reference to the other man?" prompted Collins.

Cousens looked as if he were no longer in the courtroom. His gaze was fixed. The formally erect, confident man had slipped into a thousand-mile stare.

"He was an Australian and they beat him to death . . .," Cousens' voice broke. His head lowered. The poised, handsome man with the trim, military stance was crying. It was painful to watch. People looked away. They were confounded. The witness cried alone. No handkerchiefs appeared in the jury box as they had in response to Marshal Hoot's letter.

Cousens was confounded, too. Men trained at Sandhurst don't break down like that – not in public, surely – not amongst strangers. What had happened to the stiff upper lip? What had gone wrong?

"Was he a soldier?" asked Collins quietly.

DeWolfe and Knapp, attracted by the silence from the witness stand, suspended what they were doing and watched the witness.

"Yes, sir . . . He had stolen a can of onions," responded Cousens, pulling his shoulders square again.

"Who beat him?"

"Two Japanese held him while a third beat him."

"Where did they beat him?"

"They had stripped his shirt off and they beat him across the back, and then when he was on the ground, on the ankle bones and on the kneecaps in order to bring him to his feet again. Each time he got to his feet, they would beat him down again. He kept on getting up."

"Did the man die?"

"Later, when he didn't get up again, the man (Japanese) grunted at us to take him away. We did, and he died before they could get him on board ship."

DeWolfe asked Judge Roche to excuse the jury so that counsel could argue the issue of duress. The judge so ordered and the jury filed out of the courtroom.

James Knapp felt his way into the argument for the prosecution.

"The evidence here, the most that can be said about it is that this witness communicated those facts and told those horrible details to the defendant, but that is not force exercised upon the defendant . . . Unless and until he can show that there is some duress upon the defendant . . ."

"He indicates and assures the Court," said Roche, "That this course of conduct was communicated to the defendant."

Knapp saw the definition he was after.

"Your honor, I do not believe . . . that even if the course of conduct was communicated to her that it would constitute a duress here."

Judge Roche was not convinced.

"Not in itself, it would not," he replied to Knapp, "but it would be hard for anyone to determine that it was not an element of coercion."

Cousens assured the Court that "every one" of the facts being related by the witness was communicated to the defendant.

DeWolfe interjected, "It is too remote from the issues, too long before he went to work there and before he met her, not proper."

Olshausen joined in the defense argument.

"The point is the imminence of the threat and the seriousness of the threat depends upon how many facts there are to induce it. Of course . . . it is a matter of degree . . . you don't get the full force of the threat until you put in all the evidence. We have started with this witness. This is the beginning of the proof."

Knapp responded for the prosecution.

"We can see the course that the testimony will take. We hesitated to raise this issue until this time when we were certain where we were going with it. The force must be immediate and upon the person of the defendant . . . The fact that force was used on somebody else doesn't necessarily mean it is going to be used on her . . ."

Judge Roche responded to Knapp.

"You charge she was part of this transaction. Both of them (Cousens and Iva Toguri) were broadcasting."

Knapp moved his argument to the time element.

"Well, these events took place months before, even a year and a half before she ever broadcast. Conditions might have changed in that time."

Judge Roche replied, "That would be a question of fact for the jury."

The court broke for lunch, and DeWolfe plotted out the line of argument the wished to take during the afternoon

"I want to go further with respect to the order of the proof," Knapp resumed the argument before Judge Roche. "As I understand, Mr. Collins' proposition here is that by asking the simple question, 'Well, did you later communicate this to the defendant?' that he straightened out his order of proof. I do not think so. My objection goes until . . . there is some showing that she was threatened or under fear of force by some Japanese authority there at Radio Tokyo, and an immediate fear, and until there has been some showing with respect to that, this evidence is improper and out of order."

Judge Roche agreed, "I think we are confronted with a problem of order of proof, and at this time, I shall sustain the objection."

Knapp pressed his new advantage.

"If your honor please, may it be understood the objection and ruling goes to this entire line of testimony, and I would like . . . to move that the testimony of the witness as to events occurring during his capture in Malaya should be stricken and that the jury would be instructed to disregard it . ."

Judge Roche sustained the line of argument for the prosecution. Cousens was not allowed to relate any force or threat of force used against him by the Japanese.

At Kempei tai headquarters in Tokyo, Cousens testified, he was knocked about by a Japanese in civilian dress. The prosecution objected. The objection was sustained.

At Radio Tokyo, as a result of his written protest, Cousens testified how he was forced to stand at attention and bow before Tsuneishi, face with an unsheathed sword as Tsuneishi read an order. The prosecution objected. The objection was sustained.

Collins proceeded in his questioning to that time when Cousens had met Iva Toguri (August of '43), and proceeded doggedly to establish the close relationship of the defendant's broadcasting to the starved condition of the PWs.

On the morning of the second day of direct examination, Judge Roche pressed for closure.

"We have had this witness on the stand for a day and a half," advised Judge Roche.

"I know, your honor, but I think he is our most material witness, because he was at Radio Tokyo with the defendant," responded the defense attorney.

Collins proceeded in detail to have Cousens spell out the aid which Iva Toguri had given to the PWs which had made her help so valuable. Prosecution objections were temporally stilled, but not for long.

The prisoners at Bunka Camp, testified Cousens, ". . were in very poor condition; we badly needed medicine . . . citrus fruit, I recall, because the men had pellagra."

Collins: "Anything else?"

Cousens "Yes, sir . . I gave her (Iva) some money and asked her to see what   she could do to buy those things . ."

Collins: "Did she?"

Cousens: "Yes, she did."

Collins: "More than once?"

Cousens: "Regularly."

Collins: ". . . On how many occasions did she produce food for you?"

Cousens: "Scores of times, sir."

Collins: "Who consumed that food?"

Cousens: "I did, Ince did, occasionally Reyes, and we took some of it into Bunka Camp with us."

Collins: "Did you have your regular rations at Bunka Camp?"

Cousens: "No, sir. The fact that we had this food at Radio Tokyo enabled us to forego our rations which had been drawn for us at Bunka, and they were given to the other men."

Collins: "Did you pay the defendant or did anyone else pay the defendant for all   the food that she purchased for PWs?"

Cousens: "No, sir."

Collins: "Did she purchase other things besides food for you?"

Cousens: "Yes, vitamin pills . . tobacco, and a blanket on one occasion."

Now, prosecution resumed its objections. The defendant's aid, said Knapp, "doesn't go to the intent to commit an act of treason at all. It only shows she might be a kindly, kind-hearted person."

Knapp's objection was sustained.

Cousens went on to testify that he had informed the defendant of the conditions of the war prisoners.

Knapp spoke up again. "Object, your honor. The question of the reason for which she gave food and medicine is immaterial. The fact is she gave it. The reason for which she gave it is of no concern."

Knapp's objection was sustained. From that point on, the trial record was maintained as if the defendant's aid to the PWs was not related to her intentions in broadcasting as Orphan Ann.

Incredibly, the significance of Iva's actions in aiding the PWs had been tossed aside as if it were of no consequence!

"I guess I should have jumped up and shouted, 'No, I'm not a kind-hearted person!' I should have done <u>something</u>," acknowledged Iva. *"But I was so dumbfounded, I just sat there. I couldn't believe it."*

One avenue still open to the defense on the issue of intent was the intent of Cousens in selecting Iva Toguri as his confrere on Zero Hour, and his instructions to her. Collins pursued that line of questioning and Cousens responded at length.

"As near as I can remember, I said to her, 'Here is tonight's script, Ann. Now, I want you to read in this way. You will notice we have got a satirical bit her about 'Strike up the Band'. Take that sergeant's part tough, like this . . . in that next part, take it very light, rather 'sissy', and I would have done that for her because it was specific reference to a comic record . . . then, to come in very fast on what I explained to her was what we called a 'wipe' in radio terms.

"If you have a commercial program and the commercial has just been read, if the next unit on the program jumps in fast, you get entirely the wrong effect from what the sponsor wants, because the listener's mind is jerked away from what has just gone on, and you get, in effect, a 'wipe' (erasure) . . . I explained to her many times to pick this up as soon as the 'Home Front News' was over, not to say just 'Thank you', and into the program, but 'Thank you, thank you, thank you, thank you', and it was written in here a multiplicity of times, to jump in and take that fast . ."

Cousens then read the script as he had instructed the defendant to read it:

"Hello, there, enemies. How is tricks? This is Ann of Radio Tokyo, and we're just going to begin our regular program of music, news and the Zero Hour for our friends – I *mean* our enemies in Australia and the South Pacific. So, be on your guard and mind the children don't hear? All set? Okay, Here's the first blow at your morale, the Boston Pops playing 'Strike up the Band'"

There was no doubt about the skills of the performer or of his ability to weave double meaning into the script he was reading, but Judge Roche didn't appreciate the show. Eventually, he interrupted.

Court: "Is that all from this witness?"

Collins: "No, no, your honor, I want to get to some further explanations, because these require explanations."

Cousens took up the Orphan Ann script of March 9, 1944, "I recall this phrase which occurs here, 'That's not bad atoll, atoll'; and I coached her in that and coached her . . . because that was a reference to the island hopping that was going on . . . that's not bad atoll, atoll; all right boys, one more left and then you can have your beer."

The meaning behind his instructions to the defendant, concluded Cousens on direct examination, was "to sabotage" the Japanese purposes "in every way possible". He had chosen Iva Toguri as Orphan Ann, said Cousens, because she had a "gin-fog voice – I hope I can say this without offense", which was what he needed to make "a complete burlesque" of the propaganda content on the Zero Hour.

The prosecution's cross and recross examinations were very brief. They did nothing to shake the credibility of the witness.

For once, DeWolfe met a witness who was as quick to grasp a rhetorical opening as DeWolfe was:

DeWolfe: "Any other Japanese bring you food besides the defendant?"

Cousens: "The defendant was not Japanese. She was an American."

Except for the one breakdown under friendly, direct examination, Cousens left the witness stand without having any difficulty whatever.

CHAPTER XXIV
THE SILENCED PWs

Wallace E. (Ted) Ince, the next defense witness, was under the threat of indictment and knew it. He was accompanied to court by his attorney, A.J. Zirpoli.

At first, the tall red-haired major was very composed. He was back to his normal weight. He spoke tersely, unemotionally. Then came a series of sympathetic questions from Collins about treatment of the PWs at Bunka Camp.

"We were beaten, starved, subjected to indignities . .," said Ince.

Then, the tall, noncommittal witness stopped and buried his head in his hands. Sobs racked him. His shoulders heaved as he tried to control himself.

Again, people stared and then, looked away. After what seemed a long time in the hushed courtroom, Ince spoke again.

"It is not so easy . . . it is not so easy to talk so matter of factly of brutality. It is quite a different thing . . ."

The prosecution objected, saying that the witness was not relating what happened.

Ince responded sharply: "I am telling what happened . . . Men you knew well, lived with, worked with, fought with, died horribly."

Like Cousens, said Ince, he had broadcast under threat of death. His life was threatened frequently by Lt. Hamamoto, by George Uno, and by Tsuneishi.

Ince testified that Iva Toguri's aid to him had included eggs, noodles, rice, vegetables, fruit, vitamin pills, tobacco, the woolen blanket that Cousens had mentioned, and almost daily news of Allied victories.

"The PWs were all hungry – always," Ince concluded.

On cross examination Ince told of an initial reaction of distrust when Cousens first wanted to include Iva Toguri as confrere on the Zero Hour.

"I told him (Cousens) I didn't like it. We had a working agreement between the three of us (Cousens, Ince, and Reyes), and I didn't want to take chances on Toguri."

Knpap: "You didn't trust her."

Ince: "Certainly not."

Knapp: "Then, you don't know whether she was ever part of that
agreement?"

Ince: "I believe she was."

The third and last of the three war prisoners from Zero Hour looked tall and handsome again, and still young enough for teenage spectators to identify with. Norman I. Reyes, widely publicized as a star prosecution witness since March of '48, had mustered his courage to testify for the defense. During the first day of his testimony, it appeared that the defense had found it model witness.

Asked about the defendant's loyalty to the United States, Reyes testified:

"I would put my life in her hands. She was part of the PW plot to sabotage the Zero Hour," Reyes added, and explained that he also was the recipient of food, medicine, tobacco, and new items from her.

Then came the cross examination, and the roof caved in on the suave and handsome young man.

Reyes was confronted with five FBI statements in the hands of Tom DeWolfe, all bearing his signature.

Reyes had not told Collins about the statements to the FBI.

In the statements appeared direct contradictions to just about everything that Reyes had just stated as a defense witness, i.e.: He, Reyes, was never under duress to broadcast at Radio Tokyo; Cousens wanted a benevolent Japan to dominate the Pacific; Ince had broadcast because of "inducements of better living quarters and more freedom"; Reyes knew of "no threats, duress or coercion that was exercised or directed to influence Iva Toguri" in her broadcasting; and no conspiracy or plot had existed among the PWs to sabotage Japanese purposes on Zero Hour.

Confronted with the signed statements, Reyes blurted one obvious truth, "I would have signed anything to get out from under."

He elaborated: "I could see them building up overt acts, and I thought if overt acts was all that was needed for a case of treason, I might be as guilty as the defense."

Reyes did not break down – shed no tears on the witness stand. But he left the defense in shambles, temporarily.

If Collins had known about Reyes' statements to the FBI, the Filipino never would have been called to the stand.

The next PW witness for the defense was one of the two men thought, until near the end of the war, to have been executed at Bunka Camp, Captain Edwin Kalbfleish, Jr.

Kalbfleish had ad-libbed on a script over a microphone at Radio Tokyo, had been slapped away from the microphone, and hustled off by guards, never to be seen again by the other prisoners at Bunka. Guards had made a show of discarding his clothing and bedding as "not needed anymore."

Kalbfleish felt that he owed his life to the moral courage of Tamotsu Murayama, who intervened with Tsuneishi to send Kalbfleish to another prison camp, rather than to execute him. (Ironically, one might infer, it was possible that Murayama also saved Tsuneishi a war crimes charge. It would have taken only one documented execution of a PW at Bunka Camp to have put Tsuneishi before a War Crimes tribunal.)

On direct examination Kalbfleish got into the record that, "Cousens is the type of man we would have followed through hell."

But Kalbfleish wasn't allowed to testify about aid that he had received from the defendant (prior to having been sent to another prison camp) because he had not received it directly from her hands – it had passed through other PWs hands. Along that line of questioning, Kalbfleish sat on the witness stand for 15 minutes without being allowed to speak a word, due to sustained objections from the prosecution.

The argument between counsel became bitter. The judge showed anger as well. His jaw was set.

Collins: "If your honor please, as to the offer of proof, I want simply to state in substance what the testimony was that I failed to elicit from the witness in response to those questions."

DeWolfe: "I do not think that is necessary."

Court: "What was that?"

Collins: "I said I would like, now, to state in substance . ."

Court: "I suggest to you that you record for all purposes."

Collins: "Do I understand by that, your honor is indicating that we are not to be permitted to show the exact answers here?"

Court: "The witness is on the stand. You examine him in any manner you see fit."

Collins: "I have concluded my examination of the witness. My only purpose is to ascertain what the answers of the witness would be to those questions in order to make a proper order of proof."

Court: "You will have to develop that from the witness stand."

Collins: "Then, I understand your rulings are against us."

Court: "There is nothing before the Court. Proceed."

After Kalbfeish left, three other Bunka Camp PWs appeared for the defense on the witness stand, Australian Kenneth Parkyns, American Army Major Willesden Cox, and U.S. Naval Ensign George E. (Bucky) Henshaw. All were muted on the stand because of direct contact with the defendant. Henshaw had suffered beatings, withdrawal of his food allowance due to "poor performance" in script writing, and extra calisthenics when he already could hardly stand on his feet.

The key deposition offered by the defense was that of PW Nicholas Schenk, the Dutch Army lieutenant who had served as cook at Bunka Camp. The deposition is outlined as follows (explained in further detail on pages 98-100):

"We had a speech every day for two or three months," Schenk had testified, "intended to break us down mentally and to force us to believe that there was no way out – one line I particularly remember is that 'nothing is guaranteed'. Tsuneishi told us the wall, which we saw around us, could be climbed easily, but anyone who did it would come back in pieces."

"The daily diet for the PWs, said Schenk, consisted of "three tea cups of corian per day, a kind of corn . . . to fill the bellies of chickens, and its effects were severe beri beri and pellagra; and three bowls of soup to get that down with. The bowls were a little larger than the tea cups. The soup consisted of dikon, which is horseradish, a little salt, a little soya, to which water was added."

All of the PWs had malnutrition, said Schenk, and he named individuals and their ailments.

"McNaughton had boils. Major Cox was flat on his back for three months, not able to move. Larry Quilly lost 40 pounds in about six months. I suffered diminishing eyesight and, later, leg deterioration. All of us had beri beri. Kalbfleisch and Streeter also had temporary blindness. Larry Quilly lost his hair."

"Cousens and Ince," Schenk had continued to Tamba in the deposition, "brought some foodstuffs they got from Radio Tokyo. An old lady and her husband living in the basement of our quarters were sent once in a while to get us some food items, and we collected the young leaves from the trees, which had been proven edible in Singapore. I, personally, killed two cats. Frank Fujita killed another couple of cats, and we consumed them. We ate at least two dogs."

The PWs were slapped around by Japanese officers, said Schenk. "Larry Quilly was beaten repeatedly. Ince was beaten severely. Henshaw was beaten, also Parkyns, Shattles, and myself. Lt. Hamamoto, a sergeant from the Kempei tai, Uno, another Japanese named Hishikara, and Endo beat us. Ikeda never beat PWs. Ince, weighing 130 pounds, was called out to do exercise by the Kempei sergeant. Ince had to bend his head low and that made him dizzy. He couldn't get up. Hanamoto ran out from his room into the courtyard directly up to Ince and knocked him out. Ince was unconscious for a few minutes. I know Hamamoto's swing . . . pretty severe because he knocked me out, myself, when I complained about food, and it took me four days to recover from that."

At one point in the deposition Schenk had described Tsuneishi as "smart, sword rattling, and arrogant, with an inferiority complex before white men."

In reading of Schenk's deposition, however, a fantastic legal tangle developed. DeWolfe had barraged the defense presentation of the deposition with 87 sustained objections, and then had refused to offer the cross examination. Collins then offered the prosecution's cross examination in the interest of the defendant.

Court: "I have never run into this situation before."

DeWofe: "I never have either, sir."

Collins: "Neither have we . . ."

Eventually, DeWolfe did not contend with the defense's right to offer the cross examination, but he then objected 60 times (to more than 75% of the questions), and all 60 objections were sustained.

DeWolfe managed to keep out of the Court record all testimony that had occurred on cross examination about the starvation diet and physical abuse by guards of prisoners at Bunka, while at the same time protecting his legal situation by conceding that the entire deposition had to be considered if the defense wished that it should be.

Collins, by his insistence upon reading, question by question, the prosecution's cross examination, got most of the words of Nicholas Schenk spoken in the presence of the jury. The jury, of course, was told to ignore them, but that didn't change the fact that they had heard them.

Next, the exhausted jury heard from a few of the U.S. ex-servicemen in the Pacific who had enjoyed Orphan Ann and remained uninjured psychologically either by Ann or all of those other Roses.

In a trial by legend, what should the prosecution do with that part of the legend which pre-dated any action of the defendant on radio? Obviously, Iva Toguri should have been vindicated from any association with the earlier broadcasts. But she was not!

CHAPTER XXV

BRIBERY RULED IRRELEVANT

In the ornate courtroom of Judge Roche, Wayne Collins dangled a suit of clothing – the rumpled suit which Brundidge had given to Hiromu Yagi's friend, Tosh Kodaira, in Tokyo. The suit was monogrammed with Brundidge's full name in pants and coat. After nine weeks of trial, Collins dangled the suit before the jury like a skeleton from the prosecution's closet and offered Tosh Kodaira's deposition in evidence.

The deposition told the full story from the time that Hiromu Yagi had phoned his friend, Kodaira, saying, "Tosh, don't you want a trip to the United States?" – to Kodaira's refusal of the free trip and his lecture to Yagi in a Tokyo teahouse about the grave implications of perjury.

The prosecution objected.

With the jury excused, Olshausen for the defense and DeWolfe for the prosecution argued before Judge Roche. The deposition, said DeWolfe, was based upon hearsay and should not be allowed in evidence because it focused upon two people who had not appeared as witnesses in the trial (Yagi and Brundidge). Olshausen argued that Mr. Brundidge made his trip to Japan at the expense of and representing the U.S. Justice Department and that the prosecution was accountable for Brundidge's actions with Yagi and Kodaira in Japan, in March of '48.

"Mr. Brundidge," said Olshausen, "said he made the trip at the request of Attorney General Tom Clark, telling him, "Give me five days in Japan, and I can find all of the witnesses you need'." [1]

At the conclusion of the argument, Judge Roche ruled that the deposition of the witness, Kodaira, was hearsay.

Then, Collins insisted upon representing the deposition, question by question, in the presence of the jury so that the Court might rule upon each answer by Kodaira as admissible or not.

As the lengthy process started – Tosh Kodaira's deposition ran 22 pages – DeWolfe objected to every question. After 46 sustained objections, Judge Roche stopped the reading of the deposition.

"Is there any doubt in your mind counsel," said Judge Roche to Wayne Collins, "that this is not hearsay testimony?"

". . . It is my frank opinion," answered Collins, "that it is clearly admissible testimony . . ."

"It is hearsay!" asserted the judge. "Now, you have a record on it, and it seems to me it is sufficient for all purposes. I don't want to deny you any legal position that you take here in this case, but it is obvious to me, and I think it should be to you, that this is clearly hearsay testimony. I say that advisedly to you."

"Well," responded Collins in mild tones, "I have no alternative . . . save and except to read the deposition, to have your Honor make what rulings your Honor sees fit to make."

On and on the reading of the deposition went. The final score stood at 160 objections by the prosecution, all sustained (43 of the 160 on cross and recross examination); a total of 39 answers allowed, none of which related to Brundidge's or Yagi's propositions and gifts to Tosh Kadaira.

Although the deposition failed to win the favor of the Court, it impressed some of the trial reporters. Phil Hanley of the San Francisco *News* located Harry T. Brundidge at the Monterey Country Club. Brundidge acknowledged over the phone to Hanley that he had given both Yagi and Kodaira suits of clothing in March of '48, but denied that the gifts had anything to do with negotiations for testimony.

"I didn't see any sense giving a suit to Kodaira," Hanley quoted Brundidge as saying to him on the phone, "The coat hung below his knees. He wanted it anyway. So, I gave it to him. He was very grateful and brought me a beautiful 200-year-old bowl, worth twice as much as the suit when the suit was new." [2]

Ted Tamba recalled from his talks with Kodaira in Japan that Kodaira had given Brundidge a scroll, not a bowl.

The baggy, woolen suit, purchased from D & J Williamson, Inc., St. Louis, Mo., with the name, "Harry T. Brundidge", inside the vest and in the left rear pocket of the pants, was never allowed into evidence.

As for the question of who sponsored Harry Brundidge's trip to Japan in March of '48, the answer was in his passport. The visa was issued for the dates of March 4 to May 4, 1948, signed by J.D. Scott, Lt. Colonel, General Staff Corps, with this notation:

> "Object, official business for the Department of Justice"

John B. Hogan, the special assistant to the Attorney General, who accompanied Brundidge on that trip to Japan, later testified, "I had nothing to do with Mr. Brundidge's arrangement. I don't know anything about them."

CHAPTER XXVI

A HUSBAND'S VIEW OF ORPHAN ANN

Between November of '43 and May of '44, Felipe (Phil) d'Aquino had heard broadcasts of Zero Hour on an average of four times a week. Between May and October, '44, he had heard most of the broadcasts, but only the defendant's part of the program. Between October, '44, and August, '45, he had heard broadcasts on an average of one a week or less.

"What did he hear" asked Collins.

"During the course of hearing all of these broadcasts," answered d'Aquino, "I never heard one damaging remark against the Allies." [1]

Phil d'Aquino's testimony for the defense reinforced the fact that the prosecution could not possibly have chosen a better time than October, 1944, to accuse Orphan Ann of treasonous remarks on the radio. At that time, Cousens was hospitalized, off of the Zero Hour. Ince, though still at Radio Tokyo, had been transferred to another program. And Phil d'Aquino no longer had been listening to any appreciable number of the Orphan Ann broadcasts. Further, the U.S. Government seemed to have thrown away all of its recordings of Orphan Ann for the month of October, '44.

In all other matters, small, smooth-featured Phil d'Aquino was a storehouse of information about the life of the woman who had become his wife in Japan.

"We ate supper around 9:00 or 10:00 every night on week days," he said. "In the morning we had to be up at 5:00 to catch the six o'clock train to Tokyo."

Why the long train ride? Collins wanted to know.

"Well, because," explained the witness, "I had previously warned my folks that Japan was going to lose the war and that raids on major cities would be inevitable. My folks sold the house in Yokohama, and moved out. I suggested to the defendant that we move out, too, and we did. We commuted to Tokyo from Atsugi together."

It became apparent that Phil d'Aquino was one of the best informed persons in Japan on that nation's wartime predicament.

"I worked at the English section of *Gaishin* (foreign new department at Domei's central office), he testified. "To this department came all sorts of war news, Allied as well as Axis – reports form AP, UP, Reuters, and U.S. Government bulletins broadcast by the U.S. Department of Chungking and intercepted by Tokyo. Axis reports were from DNB and Trans-Ocean News Agency mostly. We also received cables from our correspondents in neutral countries such as Lisbon, Stockholm, Geneva, and also from Moscow."

Had he passed the information on to Iva Toguri after she had quit work at Domei in December of '43? Phil was asked. He answered, yes. And had she passed the information to the war prisoners? Yes, d'Aquino replied.

Collins: "Do you know of your own knowledge, Mr. d'Aquino, whether the defendant communicated to the PWs news concerning the Allies?"

d'Aquino: "Yes, I do, sir."

Collins: "Over what period of time . .?"

d'Aquino: "Around August of 1943 to the end of the war, sir. Whenever there was any important news, my wife would give that information to the PWs." [2]

About his wife's exclusive interview with Lee and Brundidge at the Imperial Hotel in 1945, d'Aquino's memories differed markedly from Lee's.

"One (Lee or Brundidge) asked, 'Are you Tokyo Rose?' and this was addressed to my wife, and my wife said she was not. And then she told them there were many women, approximately a half dozen women who had broadcast on the Zero Hour."

D'Aquino recalled none of the inflammatory "quotes" concerning 4F's dating the wives of GIs, sunken ships, and the joys of working for the Japanese Government at Radio Tokyo, all of which had been attributed to d'Aquino's wife by Clark Lee.

On cross examination of the witness, DeWolfe steered clear of questions about the Lee and Brundidge interview.

Toward the end of Collins' redirect examination of Phil d'Aquino, Judge Roche dozed off. When the judge was awakened by a prosecution objection, he asked the court reporter to re-read the question. The Court reporter did. But the question referred back to an earlier question that the judge also had slept through, and the judge had to call on the Court reporter to read the next-to-the-last question too.   In transcript, the sequence read:

Counsel: :Have you any children?"

Witness: "I have no children. I had one, but it died at birth."

Counsel: "When did that occur?"

DeWolfe: "Object to that as incompetent, irrelevant, and immaterial."

(After a silence in the courtroom, the judge woke up.)

Court: "Read the question, Mr. Reporter."

Court Reporter: "When did that occur?"

Court: :When did what occur?"

Collins: "The death of her child?"

Court: "Objection sustained."

After his testimony for the defendant, Phil d'Aquino was required to go back to Japan. The U.S. had no quota for immigrants from Portugal, and Phil had been required to sign a statement saying that he would not try to enter the United States except as a trial witness. It was not a legal statement, but he was made to sign it.

CHAPTER XXVII

ORPHAN ANN TELLS HER STORY

Interviews of prisoners were not allowed, but UP staff correspondent David Leonard had no trouble getting a story from the County Jail matrons about Iva Toguri. They were outspoken in their praise of "the little nurse".

The acting senior matron, Mrs. Catherine Howerth, told Leonard, "She's very good for the other girls. She's neat and clean . . . Anybody who is sick or needs help, she knows what should be done. Someone comes in with a cut and she'll take care of them. I have no feeling (about her trial) one way or the other, but that's the truth." [1]

Iva Toguri had to be of service to other people. She had to stay busy. During the nine months between her arrival in San Francisco and the opening of her trial, she had packed her days with work. She helped at breakfast, waiting on tables and cleaning up afterward. Then, the Marshall's van picked her up for eight hours of work from 8 a.m. to 4 p.m. in the U.S. Marshall's inner office in the Post Office Building. There, she wore her plaid suit and silk stockings.

After the trip back to the jail, she changed to regulation garb for inmates (cotton, blue check calico, with frilly undergarments of her own choosing, according to Matron Howerth) and waited on tables and cleaned up afterward at dinner. The three tables were decorated with her embroidery work – bright floral designs on the table cloths. Her leisure hours were after dinner from six to nine.

"She's quiet and friendly, not at all aggressive," Mrs. Howerth described Iva to David Leonard. "She has a very calm temperament and a wonderful sense of humor . . . Her mind is on her troubles, but she isn't burdening the rest of us with them . . . She's not a stoic or a poker face at all. But I've never seen her cry." [2]

The jurors saw nothing of the person that Mrs. Howerth had described to David Leonard, nor did they see the sharp humor that had crackled over the Pacific on Zero Hour. The jurors saw a woman confounded, forced to sit still and listen to her every word and action at Radio Tokyo mulled over and over, praised and damned, turned this way and that.

By the second week in September, if words had been dust, everyone in the courtroom would have been smothered. The trial dragged by at a glacier pace.

The defendant had been word-whipped in one investigation after another for three years. But in spite of it all, she still felt, perhaps a bit numbly, that they would turn her loose.

"I suppose I had analyzed it this way," she recalled her feelings about appearing as her own witness. *"I just had to tell the truth. My family was more worried than I was when I went on the stand. I wasn't worried about it. I thought the truth would win out. I had no intention to betray this country. If I had, I couldn't have lived with myself in that courtroom."* [3]

Jun Toguri realized that people were not seeing what his daughter really was. He could sense confusion among the jurors. Jun Toguri knew people. He understood them. It would all depend upon whether the jury could identify with his daughter's plight in wartime Japan. And the judge's rulings had stopped them from doing that.

The jury had been told repeatedly that they were not to consider the plight of the defendant in Japan. That they were not to consider the plight of the PWs as having anything to do with her . . . that they were not to consider the giving of food, medicine, tobacco, and a woolen blanket to sick and starving men as having anything to do with intent . . . that they were not to consider her stubborn insistence upon remaining an American citizen as based in intent . . . they were not to consider her year of imprisonment in Japan, the denial of a speedy trial, the denial of counsel, the denial even of charges or any cause for arrest . . . in short, that they were not to consider her . . . period!

It added up to a commandment to the jury from the bench: Don't sympathize with the defendant. Don't be soft on traitors!

That was why Jun Toguri was fearful.

As for the state of the jurors, they were thoroughly confused. Their job was becoming increasingly tougher. Each one looked for an authentic sign of innocence or guilt in the defendant.

The courtroom was full, for the first time in weeks. Iva walked to the stand in her own defense in the same old tan plaid suit, ornamented only by a silver clasp which held her black hair in place. She sat, a very small person, in a rather large chair. Everything about the rococo furnishings clashed with her plain and basic style.

Judge Roche looked weary.

Fundamentally, he was a jovial and robust soul. This was *not* the way that he would prefer to spend his days – sitting in a marble chamber, in a black robe, fighting to keep from dozing. Here was Michael J. Roche, descendant of brawny Irish immigrants who drove teams, swung hammers, drove spikes alongside the Chinese, building railroads – risen to the top of the judicial heap in the city, spending his life in costume with a stern face.

As the foundation was laid for direct examination, the witness was composed. Her voice was a bit hoarse, as she described her first look at the three war prisoners on Zero Hour at Radio Tokyo.

Hearing her voice for the first time surprised many in the courtroom. Phil Hanley of the San Francisco *News* described it as a "hack-saw voice", Charles Cousens had said a "gin-fog voice", and George Uno had referred to Iva's speech as "throaty, but a fast talker". [4] It was certainly different from the sort of adjectives that had been sensationalized in the press: "syrupy", "sexy", "velvety", "seductive", [5] and so on. And yet, in a very basic way, it *was* a sexy voice – an arresting voice – a voice that commanded attention.

Unlike the voice of William Joyce, "Lord Haw Haw" of Radio Berlin, the commanding quality of Iva's voice was not based in tension or in the discordant rasp of pent up violence and hatred. The voice of Iva Toguri held listeners in the Pacific because it had a flamboyant, jocular sound. It went rollicking along like a fast-moving train on a deep roadbed. "Let's get moving," the voice seemed to say. "Let's get on with it. What are we waiting for?"

But the voice was all tied up now. She was pushing, too eager to tell her story.

"They were shabbily dressed, in sort of a canvas material cut short at arms and legs . . . They were thin . . . had sores on their feet . . . looked like scarecrows." [6]

One by one, Wayne Collins asked her if she made any of the 41 inflammatory "quotations" put into the trial record by prosecution witnesses who had been servicemen in the Pacific.

"Welcome to the First Marine Division, the bloody butchers of Guadalcanal?"

"No."

"Your wives and sweethearts are leaving you servicemen because you are overseas too long?"

"No, I never could say that."

"Why don't you stop fighting and listen to good music?"

"Never."

"This program is dedicated to the Jolly Rogers, the 90th Bomb Group. I know you are moving from Dobodura to Nadzab, New Guinea, on January 17th, and I will have a reception committee there waiting for you?"

"No, never any mention of any island, any place."

"You boneheads in the Pacific, if you expect to get home, you had better leave now. Haven't you heard, your fleet is about gone?"

"No, nothing like that."

"Go see your C.O. Demand that you be sent home. Don't stay out in that stinking jungle and let somebody else run off with your girl?"

"Never . . ." [7]

So went her denials in response to the entire list.

In the third day, the defendant responded with little show of emotion to the questioning of Wayne Collins until she came to the recollection of a time in the fall of '44, when she was rebuked by a liaison man between radio employees and the Imperial Japanese Army. The man, S. David Huga, had picked her out as the only one at Radio Tokyo who "had failed" to support the Japanese war effort.

At last, Iva cried. Slowly, painfully, the dark eyes brimmed with tears. She daubed at them with tissue.

"I told him," she said, *"I told him he would never get an agreement out of me. I told him, 'I'll quit today; I'll take the consequences'."* [8]

Again, as had been the case with Cousens and Ince, the tears of Iva d'Aquino brought little show of emotion from the jurors.

Direct examination was summed up with a blanket denial by the defendant of all allegations made by the prosecution in the trial against her. She had not, she said, ever broadcast "any smut". . . "obscenity" . . .

"predictions concerning troop movements" . . . "any statement relating to casualties suffered by the United States or it allies" . . . or "any casualties of Japan or its allies".

On cross examination, Tom DeWolfe approached her as if she were dirt. A double negative in one of his questions set off a wrangling, nerve-jarring exchange between witness, cross examiner, defense attorney, and the judge.

DeWolfe: "You did not state in 1947 that you were not Portuguese, did you?"

Witness: "May I have that question over again?"

DeWolfe: "Yes. It is hard for you to understand?"

Witness: "You had a double negative there."

DeWolfe: "Is the question hard for you to understand?"

Witness: "I believe my answer is no."

DeWolfe: "Was that question hard for you to understand?"

Collins: "I submit that this is argumentative anyway. You did not lay the foundation, Mr. DeWolfe."

Court: "The question has been asked and answered. Let us proceed."

DeWolfe: "Was that question hard for you to understand?"

Collins: "I object to that as argumentative."

Court: "She may answer."

DeWolfe: "Was that hard for you to understand?"

Witness: "Yes, because I did not know when in 1947."

DeWolfe: "You are supposed to be the one who knows, Mrs. d'Aquino."

Collins: "Just a moment. I submit, if your Honor please, that is agumentative."

DeWolfe: "Was the question hard for you to understand? Answer my question, please."

Witness: "Yes, because I didn't know whether I had made the statement orally or in a statement." [9]

DeWolfe kept up the insistent hammering – "sandpaper questioning" Delaplane called it, in which the witness was intimidated and angered. DeWolfe was imprinting upon the memories of his listeners certain phrases about lost ships, with many questions. He was also "going fishing" in his questioning, as Fran O'Gara termed it – implying that the questioner knew more than he actually did, or had documented evidence of contradictory statements by the witness.

DeWolfe: "Did you ever broadcast about loss of ships?"

Witness: "I did not broadcast anything about the loss of ships, Mr. DeWolfe."

DeWolfe: "Never did."

Witness: "Never."

DeWolfe: "Never in July, 1944, did you broadcast about the loss of ships?"

Witness: "July?"

DeWolfe: "Yes."

Witness: "Not that I recall."

DeWolfe: "What is that?"

Witness: "No, Mr. DeWolfe."

DeWolfe: "Are you sure?"

Witness: "Yes."

(DeWolfe picked up a note.)

DeWolfe: "This note on pg. 14 of the Exhibit 15 is correct, is it, about the loss of ships?"

Witness: "May I see it?"

(Iva took the note and read it. It said merely that she had *not* broadcast about the loss of ships.)

Witness: "Yes, this is correct."

DeWolfe: "That is correct?"

Witness: "Yes."

DeWolfe: "Somebody told you or suggested that you should broadcast about loss of ships, is that right?"

Witness: "Oh, no, not to me."

DeWolfe: "Not to you. Well, you heard Mr. Nakamura testify that you broadcast about the loss of ships, didn't you?"

Witness: "Yes, I did."

DeWolfe: "His testimony is false, wasn't it."

Witness: "I don't know whether I am in the position of saying that anybody's testimony if false."

DeWolfe: "I see. Well, you never did broadcast to any American troops at any time that their ships were gone, did you?"

Witness: "No."

DeWolfe: "And 'how are you going to get home now'?"

Witness: "No, I can't . . ."

DeWolfe: "You didn't tell Clark Lee that you broadcast in 1944, 'You boys are all without ships now, you are really orphans of the Pacific. How are you going to get home now?' You didn't tell Mr. Lee   that you broadcast that, did you?"

Witness: "That's right, I didn't tell him I broadcast that."

DeWolfe: "You didn't tell him that?"

Witness: "No, I didn't tell him I broadcast that."

DeWolfe: "You heard him testify that you did tell him that."

Witness: "Yes."

DeWolfe: "Did you hear Mr. Reyes testify something about a broadcast about a loss of ships made by you in July of 1944?"

Witness: "I don't remember."

DeWolfe: "Did you hear anybody make such a broadcast as the broadcasting I am referring to?"

Witness: "No."

DeWolfe: "No such broadcast was ever made, according to your personal knowledge?"

Witness: "To my personal knowledge, no. No."

DeWolfe: "Well, somebody suggested that you broadcast to the American troops, 'You fellows are all without ships. What are you going to do about getting home? You are orphans of the Pacific now?'"

Witness: "That is what I heard two or three other people talking about. You see, Mr. DeWolfe, a lot of phrases that were used in Major Cousens' scripts were borrowed for other purposes. There were six or seven copies made, and I heard that suggestion one day when I came late to the studios." [10]

Cousens would have known exactly how to counter DeWolfe's technique of "imprinting" through repetition and suggestion. Cousens would have countered with the "wipe' technique, jamming the phrasing and the rhythms with his answers until the questioner had to re-phrase the questions. Iva d'Aquino wasn't that knowledgeable about speech techniques.

CHAPTER XXVIII

ABOUT THOSE LOST SHIPS

The whole passage concerning loss of ships conveyed no clear meaning of who had said what to whom over Radio Tokyo. Here is the complete part, with no changes in punctuation, spacing, capitalization, or spelling, just as the notes initially were recorded on September 1, 1945, in Lee's room at the Imperial Hotel:

"sometimes fighting news, admit defeat in typical german fashion, 'well planned defeat,' like seritorius. advance to the rear.' exaggerate your losses, minimize ours.

"off formosa claimed sunk american fleet. they sent major from GHQ who wanted to play up great victory wiping out u.s. fleet. i get inside news, and we add up ships claimed sunk and they wouldn't add. would be suicide say trugh. after this time, last year we just mouthpiece of ghq. they'd bluntly suggest 'you fellows all without ship. what are you going to about getting home.' 'Orphans of the Pacific. You really are orphans now.'

"about every day for past half year major come, english speaking, and tell me how to slant that day's script. when okinawa battle, japanese took back one little place, they played it up big.

'twas so funny . u.s. announce ship so many man of wars of japan; then japanese announce almost identical. trying to make them look equal." [1]

Since none of the 22 radio broadcast scripts, or parts of scripts, introduced into the trial was dated later than September 15, 1944, no actual script lines were available for the month of the alleged broadcast about "loss of ships".

Therefore, Orphan Ann's explicit broadcasts for that month of October, '44, remained conjectural.

But one need not have been in the Pacific at that time to discover what was being received from Radio Tokyo news casters. One could read it on microfilm in the New York *Times*. October of '44 was the month of the fictitious "Battle of Formosa" and of the actual second "Battle of the Philippines Sea" in the San Bernardino and Suribao Straits.

The New York *Times* of October 27, '44, reported that Radio Tokyo claimed the Japanese Navy had sunk eight U.S. aircraft carriers, three cruisers, two destroyers, four transports, and shot down 500 U.S. planes between October 24th and 26th in the "Naval Battle of the Philippines:.

Three days earlier in the *Times* (on October 24th), it was reported that the Imperial Japanese Army had forced Filipinos at Tacloban to march through town in honor of a "great Japanese victory over Admiral William F. Halsey's fleet off Formosa". The quotation was attributed to one of the marchers, Jose J. Brillo, Philippines official of the Provincial Treasury Department at Tacloban.

"They told us," Brillo was quoted as saying, "they had sunk seven carriers and eight battleships and downed 800 planes and that 13,000 Marines had been drowned. We knew it wasn't true, but we had to march anyway, and bow 45 degrees from the waist to the Japanese flag they put in the streets." [2]

That's what Tosh Kodaira had recalled from a San Francisco broadcaster, who had begun his news commentary with "Well, Radio Tokyo's done it again." [3]

From blitz day at Pearl Harbor to the end of the war, the Imperial Japanese Navy, according to Radio Tokyo, had sunk the U.S. fleet repeatedly.

The first Tokyo Rose "quote" recorded in a U.S. submarine log had claimed the total destruction of the U.S. fleet:

"Where is the United States fleet?" jeered Tokyo Rose, introduced by a jiu jitsu rendition of 'It's Three O'Clack in the Morning', "I'll tell you where it is boys . . It's lying at the bottom of Pearl Harbor." [4]

Next, according to Radio Tokyo, the Japanese Navy had won a great victory and the "remnants of the U.S. fleet" were being pursued and destroyed at the Battle of the Coral Sea. And then again at the Battle of Midway.

Then, in October of '44, the U.S. fleet was reported destroyed again in the "Battle of Formosa", and still again once more in the "Naval Battle of the Philippines".

By that time, Japanese listeners to Radio Tokyo were beginning to wonder why it was necessary to destroy the United States fleet so many times. It was reportedly asked: "Where would Radio Tokyo report the sinking of the U.S. fleet next? In Yokohama Harbor?"

The only document entered at the trial to relate Iva d'Aquino to a news comment over Radio Tokyo about loss of ships was the entry in Clark Lee's news notes.

It was a pompous style that made Radio Tokyo's propaganda so ludicrous, and it was exactly that style which had been lampooned so well by Cousens in the Orphan Ann scripts, for example, "Please to listening, honorable enemies . . . You are listening, please?" This would be contrasted with a sudden break into American idiom, such as "Where the hell's that Orphan choir? . . . Oh, there you are . . . this is Ann here! . . . How about singing for me tonight? You won't! . . . All right, you thankless wretches, I'll entertain myself and you can . . ." [5]

Orphan Ann's lines and style were a hit among the "Orphan family" because they grew out of the war context. Without some knowledge of what was going on in the Pacific at the time, the comic impact was lost.

In no way could Iva Toguri bring into perspective, in court, the comic impact of her role as Orphan Ann on Zero Hour over wartime Radio Tokyo. Under the relentless cross examinations of Tom DeWolfe, it had seemed a far-fetched idea that there could be anything funny about the wartime broadcasting of Orphan Ann.

DeWolfe: "You did not think the Japanese, Mrs. d'Aquino, were paying you to get up and entertain American troops, did you?"

Witness: "That is what they were doing."

DeWolfe: "That is what they were doing. You honestly, Mrs. d'Aquino, and sincerely thought the Japanese were paying you money to entertain American troops, is that right?"

Witness: "No, that is not right."

Having been stripped of her alliance with the war prisoners of Zero Hour on the key issues of duress and intent, Orphan Ann was also stripped of her only official commendation from the U.S. Navy.

Wayne Collins offered into evidence the tongue-in-cheek "Navy 'Citation' for Tokyo Rose of Radio Tokyo", which had been issued for release on the day that the A-bomb was dropped on Hiroshima, August 7th of 1945. It praised Tokyo Rose for "meritorious service contributing greatly to the morale of United States armed services in the Pacific". [6]

Judge Roche ruled it out of the trial record.

After five days on the witness stand, the time about equally divided between questioning from Wayne Collins and toughest kind of grilling by Tom DeWolfe, Iva burst into tears and stepped down. Collins' last question had brought the tears.

Collins: "Do you still want to be an American citizen?"

Witness: "Yes . . . that's why I made all those applications."

For ten weeks, practically the entire summer of '49, the trial reporters, the jury, Bailiff Herbert Cole, and Judge Roche, had sat through a couple of million words of testimony – a million of which were in the trial record, and another million or so which had been ruled out. The most frequently mentioned name in the trial had been Tokyo Rose.

On September 22nd, with closing arguments in progress, U.S. District Attorney Frank Hennessy was addressing the jury. Everyone was tired – only half listening to the steady flow of words.

Then it happened – the exclusion of Tokyo Rose!

"I don't think the element of 'Tokyo Rose . . . who is Tokyo Rose?' is of any importance in this case. Nobody broadcast from Radio Tokyo under the name of Tokyo Rose. Apparently, it was simply a name given facetiously by the GIs to some woman announcer of Radio Tokyo. We are more concerned in this case with Orphan Ann . . . than with Tokyo Rose.." [7]

CHAPTER XXVIX

THE VERDICT

Missing in action, completely churned out of the trial record, was the GI Tokyo Rose, the strictly-for-laughs style, the outlandish whoppers. Instead, the words flow on and on . . .

Judge Roche read to the jurors the fifty pages of instructions for the four-line crime of treason.

Here and there, something vivid popped out of the verbage. Thirty-one pages into the instructions, the topic of food was injected into a little story, a story about a good-hearted person who stole a car to deliver food.

"Good motive is never a defense where the act done is a crime. If a person does intentionally an act which the law denounces as a crime, motive is immaterial.

"Let me illustrate. I belong to a benevolent society – one that feeds the poor. The organization is badly in need of an automobile to make deliveries of food. This circumstance induces me, moves me to steal an automobile from my neighbor. My motive is a laudable one, but the intent is an entirely different matter. I intend to steal, commit larceny, and it is no defense at all to a charge of larceny that my motive was praiseworthy." [1]

The defense protested that the theoretical crime in the story did not fit the case on trial, but that the use of food in the story made it seem as if it applied directly to the situation in which the defendant had aided prisoners at Radio Tokyo and Bunka Camp.

The objection was overruled.

Two pages later in the instructions, the topic of food arose again. The Court was explicit about what was not sufficient to justify the excuse of coercion or duress:

"The fact that the defendant may have been required to report to the Japanese police concerning her activities is not sufficient. Nor is it sufficient that she was under surveillance, it is not sufficient that the defendant thought that she might be sent to a concentration or internment camp or that she might be deprived of her food-ration card." [2]

Shortly before noon on the 60th day of trial, September 26, 1949, the six men and six women of the jury filed to the jury room to reduce all of the words to one or two: "guilty" or "not guilty". The discussion would be private. They were to speak only amongst themselves. When they went to their hotel rooms, they were incommunicado – telephones were disconnected, radios removed, and no newspapers allowed. They could contact their families only through the Marshall's office.

After electing as foreman the small, neat, soft-spoken certified public accountant, John Mann, the jurors voted, and split – six for conviction, six for acquittal. All were sobered by the task ahead. They had to think about a million words in the trial record, and avoid thinking about a million words which had been ruled out. They had 125 documents to allow for, and fifty pages of the Court's instructions to guide them.

Further, they had to find the defendant guilty of the worst possible crime against the U.S. or guilty of nothing. And if their verdict should be "guilty" – then they must forego all concern about the result of it. They would have nothing to say about the punishment. The punishment could range from death to a minimum of five years imprisonment and ten thousand dollars fine, at the option of the Court.

At the press table, the trial reporters voted too. They were nine to one for acquittal, with Francis O'Gara of the *Examiner* being the lone exception.

"My overriding conviction," said O'Gara, "is that, legalistically, she committed the crime of treason, but actually was not a traitor in the true sense. What she really was doing was playing both sides – trying to work for Japan and the U.S. at the same time." [3]

The single alternate juror, Aileen Catherine McNamara, was excused and joined the spectators. Free to say whatever she wanted, she was outspoken for the defense.

The courtroom remained crowded.

In the jury room, a man and a woman who were already talking as a team, both strong for conviction, suggested that all the jurors "rule their emotions out". The judge's instructions, they emphasized, said that "the law does not permit jurors to be governed by sympathy, prejudice, or public opinion." [4] The other jurors agreed. They proceeded with their emotions, presumably, ruled out.

Nevertheless, as the jurors went through the Court's instructions, John Mann noticed considerable feeling for acquittal – a feeling which he shared.

As for the eight overt acts, John Mann recalled, "There was a general opinion that they had been committed, but the question boiled down to the sixth essential element of treason – that she must have had intent to betray the United States." [(5)]

Concentrating on their agreements, the jurors eliminated from their consideration all overt acts except numbers five and six, the two which alleged that the defendant wrote a script and broadcast about "loss of ships".

In the courtroom, as the hours passed by and no word came from the jury, the defendant appeared as anything but an inscrutable Oriental. She wept intermittently. Acquittals, she had been told, usually were arrived at quickly. She stared silently at the floor or moved restlessly to the powder room.

At 11:40 p.m., the jury gave up for the night.

The defendant went to her jail cell to weep and stare at the ceiling. Through all of the years of hardship, the year of prison in Japan, and the year that she had spent in this cell, she never had doubted that, once her story was told, she would be free. Now, her story had been told – not only told, but dragged out *as nauseum*, cried to the hovering cupids, scorned, shouted down, twisted, and tossed about like a rabbit among wolves. Now that she faced the immediate threat of conviction, uppermost in her mind was not the punishment (she didn't really believe that they would put her to death). No, the meaning of her struggle was summed up by the loss of citizenship. Convicted traitors, she knew, lose their citizenship.

"You must be in this position to realize the significance of citizenship," she was to say years later. *"Ninety-nine out of a hundred born with citizenship take it for granted, never question it. One must be pushed to the threat of losing it to realize the value, the meaning. I don't think that people realize the immeasurable value. You don't realize till you have to fight to keep it. I don't mean just of this country; I mean of any country."*
[(6)]

The next morning, Tuesday, at 9:30, John Mann again polled the jury. It stood nine to three for conviction. The nine and the three argued, and it all boiled down to all of those statements about "loss of ships". John Mann sent a note to Judge Roche, "Would it be possible for the jury to examine in the jury room the transcripts of the testimony of the following, relative to overt acts 5 and 6: Clark Lee, Oki, Mitsushio. We would prefer not to have it read to us in court as the specific passages that we would request would be indicative of the jury's present state of mind." [7]

The requested materials were sent. At 2:35 p.m., the jury was back in the courtroom. They asked for and received the entire testimony of the defendant. Eighty minutes later, they called for and got Exhibit 15, Lee's news note.

The defendant, who had to be present in the courtroom whenever the jury was, looked unsteady on her feet. Bailiff Herbert Cole kept a steadying hand at her shoulder. Clued in by the materials which the jury had requested up to then, she knew where the deliberations were centered. Win or lose, her fate was going to be decided on Overt Act 6: "That on a day during October, 1944 . . . said defendant . . . did speak into a microphone concerning the loss of ships."

In the jury room the evening deliberations heated up. The two jurors who had moved initially that all free themselves of emotions were hotter than pistols for conviction and were pressing the three holdouts (John Mann, Earl Duckett, and Edith Covell) to give in. "We've got to get this thing over with," said a majority leader, urgently. All raked through the testimony of Lee and the others, speaking in echoes of the hot arguments between defense and prosecution counsel on the courtroom floor. The minority maintained that there was a "reasonable doubt" of guilt.

A majority spokesman answered, "How would you like to be sitting out there – ten thousand miles away from home, with her telling you all your ships are sunk?" [8]

Emotions, definitely, had returned to the jury.

By late Tuesday evening, with the same nine to three deadlock still holding, the jury was ready to call it quits. John Mann sent word to the Court. Defense hopes zoomed. A hung jury would be a victory for the defense and, apparently, here it was. The Government would never foot the bill for another Tokyo Rose trial. The courtroom became quiet. Judge Roche spoke slowly, carefully:

"The jurors have reported that they are unable to reach a unanimous verdict."

He paused briefly. "The Court wishes to suggest to the jury a thought which you may wish to consider in your deliberations along with all the evidence and all the instructions previously given."

That sounded like the beginning of a speech, and so it was.

"This is an important case," the judge continued. "The trial has been long and expensive to both the prosecution and the defense. If you should fail to agree on a verdict, the case is left open and undecided. Like all cases, it must be disposed at some time."

People exchanged glances. Everyone received the message: the jury was not going to be allowed to quit.

"There appears no reason to believe," the judge went on, "that another trial would not be equally long and expensive to both sides, nor does there appear any reason to believe that the case can be again tried better or more exhaustively than it has been tried on each side. Any further jury must be selected in the same manner and from the same source as you have been chosen; so, there appears no reason to believe that a case would ever be submitted to twelve men and women more intelligent, more impartial, or more competent to decide it, or that more or clearer evidence could be produced on behalf of either side." [9]

Judge Roche now moved from budget-based argument to sympathetic concern for the jury's comfort and rest.

"You may conduct your deliberations as you choose, but I suggest to you now, retire for the night and reconvene tomorrow morning and carefully reexamine and reconsider all the evidence bearing upon the questions before you. You may be as leisurely in your deliberations as the occasion shall require, and you shall take all the time which you may feel is necessary.

"The bailiffs have been instructed to take you to your meals at any time you wish and at your pleasure, and to take you to your hotel at your own request at any time you wish, and whenever you are prepared and ready to go."

The speech ended on a kindly note indeed.

"You may now retire, ladies and gentlemen, and continue your deliberations tomorrow morning in any manner that you determine by your own good and conscientious judgment as reasonable men and women. You may now retire for the night." [10]

On the morning of the third day of deliberations, Wednesday, September 28, things got tough for mild-mannered John Mann. He was catching the brunt of the majority's attack on the three holdouts. He was holding his ground, mainly upon two quotations from the Court's instructions:

A) "The presumption of innocence is sufficient to acquit a defendant, unless the presumption is outweighed by evidence satisfying you beyond a reasonable doubt of the defendant's guilt. A reasonable doubt is a fair doubt based upon reason and common sense . . . A reasonable doubt may arise not only from the evidence produced, but also from a lack of evidence."

B) ". . . Intent to act traitorously and treasonably includes (1) specific intent to betray the United States, (2) specific intent to adhere to the enemy for the purpose of giving aid and comfort to the enemy; and (3) specific intent to give aid and comfort to the enemy." [11]

The prosecution had failed on both of those counts, Mann believed.

A majority spokesman among the jurors relied for his arguments on a different quotation from the instructions:

"Intent may be inferred, keep in mind I do not say it should from statements or admissions of the defendant outside of the court, if you find she made the statements and these need only be proved by the testimony of one witness." [12]

Not just one witness, but five of them, the majority spokesman contended, testified that Iva d'Aquino said something over the radio about loss of ships. Even if Mutsushio and Oki were discounted, his argument ran, there was Lee and there was the quote in Lee's news notes.

Nerves became frayed, wills aroused. The argument assumed table-pounding proportions. John Mann became disturbed about maintaining his moral stand and at the same time, discharging his duties as jury foreman.

The jury sent for and got another thousand pages of testimony – the defense testimony by Cousens and Ince, and the transcripts and depositions of Ruth Hayakawa, George Ozasa, and Lily Ghevenian.

After puzzling over all of that, and still no closer to a verdict, they left the jury room for the courthouse at 5:20 p.m.

Judge Roche coaxed them along.

"Ladies and gentlemen of the jury . . . I have consulted with counsel on both sides, and I have determined that we ought to have a period of relaxation. I am going to suggest to the jurors that at their pleasure they go to the hotel. There will be no need of returning here tonight. Take some time and report here at 10:00 o'clock tomorrow morning. ." [13]

But the jury went back to the jury room to deliberate, without progress, until 8:00 p.m., at which time they gave up for the night.

On the fourth day, Thursday, relations between the jurors worsened. Of the nine for conviction, four were vocal. Of the three for acquittal, none was particularly vocal. The minority were being out-talked, but John Mann did not feel they were being shown any convincing proof of guilt. The arguments boiled down, again, to the defendant's intent and to how many witnesses said they heard the defendant broadcast something about a loss of ships.

The jury sent for testimony given by prosecution witnesses Shinjiro Igarashi, Mary Higuchi, and Satoshi Nakamura, along with a list of the names of all witnesses who had appeared in the trial.

The jury watchers in the courtroom felt that this was a bad sign for the defense.

Nakamura had testified that as master of ceremonies on a Radio Tokyo program in '44 and '45, he had heard Iva Toguri broadcast.

"In substance . . 'Hello, you boneheads of the Pacific. Now that you've lost so many ships, how are you going to get home?"

Igarashi, an English instructor at Waseda Language School in Tokyo, gave similar testimony, but acknowledged that he had not actually heard such a broadcast.

Mary Higuchi, a typist at Radio Tokyo, quoted three remarks she had thought she heard the defendant broadcast: one concerning wives; another concerning sweethearts; and another about the lack of ice cream in the Pacific islands.

The fourth day of deliberations drew toward evening with no change in the nine to three lineup, except for increased fatigue and frustration on both sides.

The argument had ground down to the judge's instructions.

John Mann sent a note to the judge:

"Sir:

"The jury is at a temporary impasse relative to the full interpretation of intent and motive.

"On page 41 of your instructions, it reads, '. . . the crime of treason consists of two elements: adherence to the enemy; and rendering him aid and comfort . .'

"On pages 45 and 46 (third paragraph), 'Good motive is never a defense where the act done is a crime. If a person does intentionally an act which the law denounces as a crime, motive is immaterial.'

"Overt acts of an apparent incriminating nature, when judged in the light of related events, may turn out to be acts which were not of aid and comfort to the enemy." [15]

"What," asked John Mann, "is meant by 'related events'?"

As the judge prepared to give his answer, the courtroom had filled with people again. The defendant looked as if she might not make it through the night.

Judge Roche addressed the jury.

"In relation to your request of instructions, the Court desires to instruct you further in this regard; you are cautioned not to select a single instruction or portion of an instruction alone, but to consider all of the instructions in determining any issue in this case. It is the duty of the jury to give uniform consideration to all of the instructions herein given, to consider the whole and every part of them together, and to accept such instructions as a correct statement of the law involved.."

The judge paused.

John Mann felt rebuffed – dismayed. It was Mann who sought the clarification of the instructions.

The majority for conviction held that the matter already was clear, that their task was done – it remained only for the three holdouts to do theirs.

"It is time to go to dinner," said the judge. "I have a desire to go to dinner, and I hope the jury has. We have been working very steadily here, and I suggest to the jury, I realize how earnestly they are working, and if it is agreeable to the jury, they may come back here or they may retire to the hotel for the evening again. We have spent considerable time here, and I want to be as patient as I hope the jury is in relation to these matters. You now retire and determine what you wish to do. The jurors may retire. We will take a recess." [16]

As the jury filed out, most of the spectators left too. It looked like another evening of deliberation with no verdict.

But in the jury room, the jurors didn't want to eat or talk together any more. They had had it. John Mann felt more isolated than he ever had before. He felt that the judge's refusal to clarify instructions was a reprimand to him and a denial of the case for acquittal.

Reluctantly, the three holdouts agreed to a unanimous verdict, based upon overt act number 6, that on a day in October, 1944, Iva Toguri had broadcast something about "the loss of ships."

When the jurors returned to the courtroom, just 33 minutes after they had left, about 40 people were still there. The trial reporters took back row seats, waiting for what they supposed would be the jury's routine acceptance of the dinner suggestion.

"She was such an inoffensive little thing," John Mann recalled, "sitting there,working against herself with her impassive expression . . . I think I know how she felt because I felt the same way when I was cut off from everybody. You ask the judge a question and he reprimands you. He definitely tells you you're out of order. The count is nine to three against you. I couldn't help feeling the isolation she must have felt in Japan." [17]

As the Court Clerk read, in the very silent room, the one word, "Guilty," his voice faltered slightly.

A disappointed "oh" sounded through the audience.

Iva slumped in her seat, stared at her hands. After eight years of hell, here it was. Conviction!

Judge Roche's face was absolutely expressionless.

As people began to stir, all about Iva were expressions of shock and incredulity.

Alternate juror Aileen McNamara just kept repeating, "How could they do it? How could they possibly do it?"

Asked by Stan Delaplane, "Did you at any time consider her not guilty?" John Mann answered, "If it had been possible under the judge's instructions, we would have done it." [18]

After sampling the crowd, Delaplane noted, "It is an interesting point that most of the regular spectators who sat through 13 long weeks had concluded the girl was not guilty."

The press reaction was critical. Connie Hitchcock of INS was so indignant that she couldn't talk calmly about it.

Katherine Pinkham of AP was appalled. "Americans believe strongly in fair play," she said, "and that sense has been violated here." [19]

Paine Knickerbocker was convinced, "they have convicted her on a legend." [20]

Bill Bancroft said, "she did just about what you could expect of a loyal and reasonable person." [21]

Delaplane wrote, "the judge's instructions (or rather his lack of clarification at the end) swung them over. The acquittal forces had banked on a clarification that would enable them to hold out – and make it a hung jury." [22]

Feature writer Paul Brook of the *Examiner*, not a regular trial reporter, wrote another version of how the decision was reached by the jury:

"Two persons on the jury which convicted Mrs. Iva Toguri d'Aquino (Tokyo Rose) refused to let their emotions sway them. That was the scant margin by which she escaped acquittal on treason charges, it was learned after the jury was discharged . .

"It was the perseverance of these two jurors – one a man, the other a woman – that finally convinced the others and resulted in a verdict of guilty, 78 hours and 20 minutes after they received the case.

John Mann, the jury foreman, admitted, "After the first ballot had been taken, the jurors decided to rule emotion out, and from then on the swing toward the final verdict began.

"It wasn't easy ruling out my emotions," was the way Mrs. Ival Long, one of the jurors, explained it, "but we did it." [23]

The best a juror can do with his or her emotions is to express and assimilate them. There is no way in the world to rule them out.

The sentencing took place a week later, on October 6th, and to the further distress of John Mann, it was not the minimal sentence. Iva was condemned to 10 years in the Women's Federal Prison at Arlington, West Virginia, and fined $10,000

.

The jail matrons, the bailiff, the court reporter, and other federal employees connected with the case made it a point to express sympathy to Iva and disappointment about the verdict.

As Iva took the long train ride to Alderson, West Virginia, away up in the mountains, farther east than she ever had been in the United States before, the spirit in her rose. Stripped of citizenship, convicted of treason, starved and derided and shoved from one stateless category to another for eight long years – she was, apparently, indestructible.

"I will do the ten years," she said to Bailiff Herbert Cole, *"and I will sleep every night of it, but I don't think the same thing will be true for Mitsushio and Oki."* [24]

Herbert Cole was moved to admiration. Years later, when he had become house detective at the Sir Francis Drake Hotel in San Francisco, he told the author, "I took her off the boat, and my wife and I took her to Alderson Prison in West Virginia. There was no criminal element about her – nothing at all." [25] Cole was the man often photographed with her as she went in and out of the courtroom in her glen plaid suit. He treated her as gently as if she were his own daughter. He was with her every trial day.

"It really hurt when we had to leave her back there," he confided. "It was like leaving one of our own." [26

CHAPTER XXX

THREAT OF DEPORTATION

At the federal women's prison at Alderson, West Virginia, the arrival of Tokyo Rose brought out the usual excitement. The matrons expected someone all decked out in mink and pearls. But instead, they saw Iva in her plaid suit.

Alderson was a pleasant surprise, small and homey, with an inmate population which varied from 300 to 500, and very few hardened or vicious criminals. Most of the inmates were moonshiners, brought in from the Carolinas and the Smoky Mountains of Tennessee – in for violation of federal liquor tax laws.

Iva found some good bridge players, one of whom was Mildred (Axis Sally) Gillars.

"They ranged," Iva described the inmates, *"from women who have never before worn shoes to brilliant and sophisticated women. I found that Mildred Gillars was a brainy person. We never talk about what had happened."* [1]

To her surprise, prison time at Alderson went fast and for the most part, pleasantly.

"In a way," she said, *"I appreciated the time to myself. I always had thought that prison time would be wasted and go by very slowly. But it didn't. The flunky in me always comes out."* [2]

She became supply clerk first, then did a card study, then became assistant to the medical aide, then x-ray operator; after that, medical purchaser; and finally, laboratory assistant, in which job she ran the x-ray lab, tested Basic Metabolism Rates (the highest she ever tested was her own – a plus 84), and took electrocardiograms.

"That's why I jump around so much," said Iva, when she read her record high BMR. *"I always have bothered everybody when I want to continue or finish a job after they get tired. I can't stand to sit and watch a slow-motion operation."* [3]

The prison doctor was concerned about that, and he put her on tranquilizers to slow down the action of her heart muscles, but she couldn't stand the tranquilizers.

At Alderson, the years came and went. Her family visited often. Phil was back in Japan. It was not a full life, by no means a complete life, but it was a time away from crowds and publicity. Surely, by the time for her release, thought Iva, Tokyo Rose would have been forgotten. Maybe she could live normally again.

But the American public had not forgotten Tokyo Rose, and neither had the U.S. Government.

While at Alderson, interest in Tokyo Rose had never died – and the pattern started long before by Brundidge and Lee seemed to have no end. In the news since her release from Alderson, the same old siren imagery rose once more, with a touch of Mata Hari thrown in. Once more, Iva was in the news (and in Tin Pan Alley, too) as *the* Tokyo Rose with a voice that was "velvety", "syrupy', and "seductive".

Harry T. Brundidge had once again reinforced the pattern with an article printed in *American Mercury* in January of '54, "America's First Woman Traitor". In the article, Brundidge, in romantic prose, related how he and Clark Lee, "bathed in the yellow light of a tropical moon" on Okinawa, made their deal to search jointly for Tokyo Rose – how they flew to Japan, found Rose, and "sipped tea" while Iva eagerly confessed her treason to them, and just as eagerly signed her "confession" for Brundidge and John B. Hogan when they flew back to Japan in March of '48.

That article in *American Mercury* ended with the author fishing for another treason charge, this one against American U.S. Army Major Wallace (Ted) Ince.

"What ever happened to the Army captain who taught Rose her trade." Brundidge had concluded the article. "Instead of being tried, he was promoted to major, a rank he still holds in the U.S. Army! Name furnished on request." [4]

That was about the last piece of writing that Brundidge ever completed. According to a brief notice of his death which appeared in the Los Angeles *Times* of April 19, '61, he had gone to Santa Cruz, California, in 1955 to write his autobiography, which was about three-fourths completed when he died.

Comedian-songwriter Abe Burrows had also done his bit to promote the treason conviction in 1955, with a little banjo twanging that began, "You stuck a knife into the U.S.A., you forgot what they learned you at UCLA."

And an anonymous *Newsweek* writer reinforced the pattern with the cutline, "Tokyo Rose: a traitor gets out," printed under an unflattering photo of Iva to match the description of her in the article, "a morose girl with sharp birdlike features . . ." [5]

The force of the news pattern created by Lee, its tenacity and predominance over fact, was remarkable. Each of the trial reporters had been struck by some aspects of that phenomenon, and several had wanted to write something about it. Somehow, none of them had ever found the time.

The GI Tokyo Rose legend had vanished into that Lee and Brundidge news pattern, backed up by that somber million-word trial record. The greatest distortion of the legend was the complete lack of humor reflected in that courtroom. The essential distortion of Orphan Ann amounted to the same thing.

"I can't imagine why so much importance was placed on the program," Iva said. *"I was so insignificant at Radio Tokyo."* [4]

Indeed, she was. But she was not insignificant among the three million GIs who had shared her common vein of humor vis a vis the Zero Hour.

When she was released from the prison in January, 1956, waiting for Iva at the prison gate was an agent of the U.S. Immigration Service with a warrant for her deportation (presumably, to Japan). She knew that if she were deported as an alien, she would not be allowed to return. She was right back where she had started from before the treason trial. She became outraged.

"This is my country!" she shouted. *"I was born here. I belong here. I'm going to stay."* [5]

She went to San Francisco and Wayne Collins arranged a press conference for her in his Presidio home.

"I'm not bitter at anything," she said at the press conference. *"I never tried to hide. I insisted on being tried to bring everything out into the open.*

"When I was caught in Japan at the time of the war, I asserted my American citizenship three times. I asked the American Government to help me get home. Nothing happened. I asked to be interned by the Japanese as an enemy alien. They didn't do it.

"I was an alien all the time I stayed in Japan. Now, they say I am an alien here. But I was born in L.A., and I have always been an American citizen. I want to stay that way." [6]

The story sped out across the land via the wire services and got some attention on the new medium, television, as well as by radio and in newspapers. Once more, the grass roots were stirred by the name of Tokyo Rose, but this time her friends were doing the stirring and the grass roots reaction was turning in her favor.

CHAPTER XXXI

RE-ENTER TOKYO ROSE

When the ex-jury foreman of the Tokyo Rose trial, John Mann, learned that the U.S. Immigration Service was attempting to deport Iva Toguri, he seized upon the opportunity to clear his conscience. In a letter to U.S. Attorney General Herbert Brownell, dated March 7th, 1956, Mann requested dismissal of the deportation proceedings.

". . . The evidence presented against her was not conclusive. Although she did broadcast from Tokyo to our troops in the Pacific, and there were transcriptions and scripts in evidence to prove this, yet these statements were innocuous and did not contain the treasonable statements attributed to her.

"My feelings in this matter are of such a compelling nature that they move me to make this most respectful request – that you consider no further steps toward possible deportation proceedings." [1]

The 41st National Guard Division of Oregon, an outfit that had fought from New Guinea to the Philippines against the Japanese, invited Tokyo Rose to come as their guest to their annual reunion in Portland, Oregon, on June 17th (1956). Co-chairmen Don Cunningham and Paul Yale announced to the press that "Zero Hour" broadcasts were the bright spot of the New Guinea to Philippines campaign. The music was good . . ." [2]

The Springfield, Ohio, American Legion Post asked that the citizenship of Tokyo Rose be restored, saying in a resolution to the American Legion National Headquarters (and released to the press) that her broadcasts were, "a source of entertainment to hundreds of thousands of fighting men and did not impede the progress of the war in any manner." [3]

The U.S. Immigration Department in Washington remained silent. The deportation warrant for Iva Toguri d'Aquino remained uncancelled. No hearing was called, no further action taken, but for two years the warrant hung over Iva's head.

Finally, in 1958, the warrants' cancellation was announced by Immigration Director Bruce Barber. He was taking action, he wrote, ". in view of recent Supreme Court decisions."

Iva's parole ended the next year, on April 18 of '59.

By the year 1958 the tide of opinion was beginning to change. Copies of the GI publications of the wartime Pacific – *Yank, Stars and Stripes, Brief,* and others – were already becoming rare. Notes by the trial reporters were disappearing into cubby holes and wastebaskets. The memories of the trial principals, the reporters, the GIs, the judge and the lawyers were being eroded by the years. Already, at the close of the year, 1958, former U.S. District Attorney Francis J. Hennessy and the dashing Clark Lee were dead.

If any were to comprehend the Tokyo Rose story – the whole thing, not just the legal thing or the news thing or the political thing the first step was a big job of retrieval: of probing through the old GI publications from the Pacific; the formal, military histories of World War II; the files of many newspapers (some of which were no more – the four San Francisco newspapers were soon to be only two), and of the three wire services (AP, UP, and INS, which had become just two now, AP and UPI). Interviews could still be had with all of the trial reporters, Judge Roche, John Mann, Tom DeWolfe, FBI Agent Fred Tillman, Harry Brundidge, and Norman Reyes (who was working at a record shop in San Francisco), Wayne Collins, Ted Tamba, and George Olshausen (all of whom were still in town), and of course, Iva Toguri.

Judge Roche, then 81, was still trying cases in the Federal Courthouse at Seventh and Mission Streets when Katherine Pinkham and the author went to see him. The date was December 22, '58, just one month before the judge was to retire.

Michael J. Roche was the sort of man that grandchildren love to climb on, and can with impunity. He was a kindly and generous man – to his own kind. That was the rub. He had a restricted idea of humankind, particularly of those who rated his consideration and respect.

He told Katherine: "It's human to err – but if I had this trial to do over, I would do the same. I've always taken the simple path in life.

"I think if it wasn't for the witness from Los Angeles, the reluctant witness (Marshall Hoot), I might have considered her innocent. They pressed him to tell, and he produced that letter. I think up to that point . . . that was the turning point.

"Up to the time that fellow pulled the letter out of his pocket, with all my experience, I was up in the air as to what might or might not have happened. There were so many voices. You could couple any of them together and say that this is Tokyo Rose."

The judge paused then, looked away, and reflected upon what he had said. He concluded, "The longer I live the more I realize the shortcomings of us all – that goes for everybody, the high and the low. The human family is a study."

He seemed to be acknowledging error. Then, he turned to Katherine once more, "You know, I always felt there was something peculiar about that girl's going to Japan when she did. I always thought she might have been up to something."

How did his aside to Katherine Pinkham square with his concluding statement? It didn't. It was a simple disclaimer. Once again, the judge had taken the simple path in life.

The complete forthrightness of the man made his bias more terrible than that of a crafty bigot. It was the sort of bias that condemns its victim, but leaves no way to address it.

Out of that interview, Katherine wrote, years later in an official plea for reinstatement of Iva's citizenship, "The trial judge I think was prejudiced without know it, and very probably tipped the delicate scales with the jurors, who relied upon him as neutral guidance between opposing attorneys." [4]

CHAPTER XXXII

JOHN MANN'S DILEMMA

John Mann was alive and well, and living in Oakland – working in the financial district of San Francisco, at the same job, same firm. He was remarkably candid.

"Frankly, I don't think the prosecution ever presented anything," he said, sharing in cheerful holiday toasts in a San Francisco bar. "She may have done something wrong, but the Government didn't prove it. From the legal standpoint, I thought the Government failed to convict her."

How did he reconcile that belief with his final vote that she was guilty?

"I wrote that in a letter to relatives after the trial," he answered. "Would you like to see it?" [1]

At John Mann's comfortable home where he and his family lived in Oakland, he dug out a copy of the six-page, single-spaced letter that he had written to relatives about the trial.

According to John Mann, just about everyone in the courtroom knew where the jurors stood before they did.

"Information since obtained," he had written in the letter, "indicated that the reporters, lawyers, and court attaches already had made a fairly good analysis of each juror. They had anticipated that I would be the foreman, had figured that two others and I would go for acquittal, had picked three that would stand for conviction, and four that would follow the majority. Two of the jurors they could not figure. The alternate juror had been classed as for acquittal, and the press and defense were hoping that she would be called upon to serve, for that reason.

"The amazing part of all this is that they were far ahead of the members of the jury who, of course, had tried similar analysis. Also amazing is the fact that, as for myself, I had not made up my mind until after the judge's instructions and so did not know, regarding myself . . ." [2]

In the years since the trial, the conviction had grown upon John Mann that he was right and the majority wrong on that jury. But, actually, almost the entire jury had felt that they should free the woman. Why hadn't they been able to do it? Only two had been resolved to convict her.

Katherine Pinkham struck the note that clarified to John Mann why the jury had resolved its decisions as it did.

"After all, who wants to come out in favor of treason?" she had suggested.

John Mann responded, "That was it – that was it! . . I *wish* I stood out myself. After so long a time, though, I just wasn't thinking clearly in that jury room." [3]

Here is the conclusion to John Mann's letter to his relatives:

"I made one statement, following the verdict, to the effect that, although there was a desire on the part of a large portion of the jury toward acquittal, it was difficult to do other than we did in view of the Court's instructions. This was quoted considerably. It is a very truthful statement, and I believe it explains clearly the actions of the jury." [4]

CHAPTER XXXIII

IN RETROSPECT

The fiery defense attorney, Wayne Collins, still had his office in the Mills Tower in San Francisco, from where he was handling the cases of thousands of South American residents of Japanese ancestry (most notably, Peruvians). His clients in Peru had been kept interned longer that the Americans of Japanese ancestry were.

Collins fought actively for a reversal of Iva's conviction until his death in 1974. His early appeal to the U.S. Court of Appeals, Ninth Circuit, had been turned down.

Speaking in his Presidio apartment in San Francisco, Collins said:

"Tokyo Rose established the precedent that, in the case of anybody who works for a foreign government – whatever they do to earn their daily bread is treason. It has grave ramifications for the press. Members of the press are the ones most immediately thrown into service if a war catches them on belligerent soil. Their skills are most useful to the enemy.

"Iva is a seed. The Tokyo Rose case stopped all proceedings against the PWs. We no longer punish the PWs; we just try to rehabilitate them. The concept of duress protected them. It should have protected her. It should spread to every category of law – even contracts, negligence, etc.

"She helped the cases of the Nisei in this country. The Government threw out the anarchist hunters and started trying to solve the problems posed by these people. But the over-all effect of her conviction has been destructive to the country and will continue to be until it is reversed." [1]

Attorney Theodore Tamba had his offices with law partners on the 17th floor of the Hearst Building. He had put the author in touch with people like Nicholas Alaga and the FBI Agent who had interrogated Iva at Sugamo Prison, Frederick G. Tillman. Tamba took time to stay in touch with many of the trial principals in Japan. He did not consider the Tokyo Rose case closed.

"I hate to see the Government kick little people around," said Tamba. "I don't like a bully. I'm a Republican and I believe in the Constitution of the United States, and I don't like a Democratic Administration pushing people around.

"I think things such as the Tokyo Rose legend should be exposed to public notice. We should prevent something like it from being repeated. We should admit an error. Not only complex treason laws are involved. Something very basic and simple is involved – the sacredness of the oath in an American Court." [2]

Tamba died in 1973.

Tosh Kodaira, the UP employee who had received the suit of clothing from Harry Brundidge, like Brundidge, was dead. So was Tamotsu Murayama, the courageous AP newsman who sacrificed his own welfare in tying to aid the PWs at Bunka Camp.

Attorney George Olshausen was writing the biggest volume the author ever saw in his cellar home in San Francisco. The manuscript covered almost everything in the room except the bed, extending in huge piles of paper almost to the ceiling.

"The meaning of treason hasn't changed," said Olshausen, "it's the attitude toward it. There is an increased impatience with anyone charged with a crime against the state, a greater tendency to impose the death penalty in treason cases recently."

Olshausen cited the cases of Tomoya Kawakits, Haupt, and the Rosenbergs.

"Iva, rather than being a victim of any active bias, was trapped by a realistic view at short range. The trial was political. Everybody excused their part in it by saying that she wouldn't be hurt. Of course it could have been worse, but the theory of legal punishment is not the theory of a battle casualty. It is a very dangerous idea that she was simply a victim of war. Taking it as a strictly legal matter, they butchered her.

"What Montesquieu said of Louis XIV –'il avait plus d'ame que d' esprit' – could be applied to Iva. From an American partisan standpoint, she was certainly the most loyal person at Radio Tokyo. Her reward was a treason conviction. All the rest, having compromised loyalty, went free." [3]

It is notable that the three defense attorneys represented a wide range of political belief. Collins was liberal democrat; Tamba, a right-wing

Republican: and Olshausen, a socialist. All served without fee in defense of Iva Toguri.

On a cold new year's day, 1959, the author emplaned for Butch O'Hare airport in Chicago, to meet Iva there.

She was 43. Would she be bitter? What had the years in federal prison done to her? What would she be like now?

CHAPTER XXXIV

IVA'S THOUGHTS

There was no hate in the little woman. On a freezing cold morning, her voice fairly crackled in the air, *"Welcome to Chicago."* It was 5:30 a.m. and ten inches of snow were being plowed out of the streets.

Iva was bundled to her ears in a big cloth coat, wearing glasses with heavy brown rims, her black hair squashed down with a scarf tied under her chin.

On that miserable, grey, windy dawn, she drove skillfully through the icy streets to J. Toguri Mercantile Company, Importers-Exporters, on North Clark Street. Ten blocks up from the store, the gangster St. Valentine's Day Massacre of 1929 had occurred – seven men against a wall in a garage.

J. Toguri Mercantile Co. was closed for the New Year holidays. Iva made coffee on an old gas range in a dining area, closed off from the store by a curtain. They stocked a complete line of dry goods . . . bright, vari-colored kimonos . .

"You think Chicago is cold? You should have been in Japan. It was cold in Japan. I mean really cold. It went to the marrow of your bones. I had to wear ear muffs from November to February, got chilblains on my feet, had a series of stupid, annoying, assorted miseries.

She shuddered at the thought.

"I knew I wasn't going to die. I was a mass of mosquito bites in summer, chiblains in winter, and they ask me – don't you want to go back to Japan!"

She was still shaken about the deportation attempt against her by the U.S. Immigration Service.

"That was the topper," she shook her head in disbelief. *"I was right back where I had started."*

She handled food very carefully, never wasted it or threw edible parts away.

"I never put any importance on food," she said, *"until I had to beg, borrow, or steal it. If I see food go to waste, I sort of cringe. I don't say anything, but that doesn't stop me from thinking."*

Had the jury understood what her gift of food to the PWs had meant in that wartime setting in Japan?

"Very few Americans ever experience hunger," Iva replied. *"You can't imagine the hardship. Sometimes, even when you had food, you couldn't prepare it. The heat often failed. I got beri beri. When you have that, you can't navigate. Your legs feel like lead."*

In view of all that had happened, if she had it to do over again, would she help the war prisoners?

She nodded, yes, *"They didn't twist my arm. I wanted to do it. It was just a right thing to do. I don't really regret it. It was my mother's training, finally.*

"I suppose it's like this. Knowing the situation, if I hadn't done something, I would have a hard time living with myself. Maybe now, I'm a convicted criminal, but by golly, I sleep nights. I doubt the same would be true for Mitsushio and Oki."

What was her feeling toward them?

"I wouldn't trust them as far as I can throw the Merchandise Mart. If another war started, they would be on the other side. I don't feel any hate. They were scared. But I don't see how their testimony got through that courtroom."

She had a sense of incredulity about it all, as if it might not really have happened if it weren't for the details, the unique impressions that came to mind.

"In the November 16th issue of the Japan or Nippon Times *(1945), a Catholic chaplain at the prison (Sugamo) wrote an article reflecting on my innocence. Nothing pulled the skids out from under me as much as that did. As a new convert to Catholicism, I was impressed with the ground rules about communion, confession, and so on. You know, any confession to a priest is confidential. Well, in the first place, the priest had done all the talking at that confession or interview or whatever it was. I was simply floored. I thought the whole world had turned against me."*

The press, for the most part, she felt, were very kind to her. How about Walter Winchell, Drew Pearson, Harry Brundidge, Clark Lee? She thought over those names.

"Neither Winchell nor Pearson ever talked to me . . . never heard me broadcast . . . never wrote me directly. I don't know anything about them and I don't think they knew anything about me."

And Brundidge?

"Brundidge was different. My father blames him for the whole thing. I don't understand why he twisted things the way he did. I don't understand what he was after.

"I first saw Brundidge on the occasion of the Tokyo interview. He had approached me through Les Nakashima, whom I trusted. It never entered my mind, I never dreamed that my conduct would be in any way interpreted as wrong. Everybody who knew me knew how I felt about Japan, and how I had tried to get back to the States. Why should I need a lawyer? It never entered my head that I would . . .

"I felt no need to be reserved. I answered all of their questions. You see, they pretended to be responsible officials. They were in uniform. They gave the impression that – they said in so many words – that I would be bothered, I would be questioned repeatedly unless I talked to them; that if I talked to them, that would be all. They certainly never mentioned the word 'confession', or 'treason'. I left the room with no sense of uneasiness. I thought that I was among friends. After all, my team had won. And they were part of my team.

"Lee, I think, wasn't so bad. I might have liked him if I had known him better. They said I glared at him when I passed him in the courtroom. I don't think I glared at him. I don't think he was a bad person."

Her thoughts moved on. She had that confounded look again.

"All through this thing, I have wondered why the big hullabaloo. I have never fully grasped why the big 'to do'. I can't imagine why so much importance was placed on the program. Except for Cousens, you could go out here to any radio station in Chicago and get as good or a better staff than that one.

"Cousens was good, I mean really *good. I believe he had them fooled. They had no authority to consult, no experience of their own – and no time for research. What Cousens had taught me still worked after he was gone. His old scripts were peppy and funny – and they did make fun of what was going on at Radio Tokyo, right under their noses. But after Cousens had left, Oki and Mitsushio wrote the scripts, except for my part – I copied Cousens' old scripts, and they couldn't write! I don't know how in the world Mitsushio and Oki got in as program directors. If they had had experience allied to radio work – journalism or drama or something – that would make sense, but they didn't have anything. Their stuff read like something out of grammar school. It was a bunch of junk.*

"I didn't think of them as part of my work. Within myself, I was ridiculing them. Of course, I couldn't do that openly. The Orphan Ann thing was a perfect way to ridicule them. When they would follow me on the mike with a home front news or something, I would get a disgusted tone in my voice and say, 'Come on in . . . '

"As for what they said at the trial, I don't feel anything against them. They were scared. They used the same words exactly, right out of the indictment, like a couple of schoolboys reciting something. But I don't see how it got through that courtroom."

She took up all of the other Roses, one at a time. She had never heard the name, Myrtle Lipton, until after the war when Buddy Uno had come to her house.

"Here is the thing that put a doubt in my mind about Uno. He said, 'You figure out a way to get me back to the States and I will help you.' I saw him as a hypocrite.

"The rest of his family was in the United States. Buddy was born and raised in the U.S. He had all of the advantages of growing up here. Then, he switched to a Japanese uniform.

"As for revenge, I never give it any thought. I don't go for vendettas. There is no hate. If anything, I am more concerned about the hardships on my family. They knew nothing about what happened in Japan. They weren't involved. It would have been much easier for them if they had abandoned me. They haven't. They stuck by me."

For those who got to know Iva, there emerged an awareness of a crowning irony. Her essence was loyalty – loyalty to family, to friends, to her country. She had unusual integrity. She was not, in any sense, fragmented or warped. How did she avoid bitterness?

"Many have told me it's a wonder I remained sane, but I have never let what happened prey on my mind. My conscience is really clear. I think people come apart from inside out. My way of living tends to be solitary. I never discuss rumors. I consider them immaterial to my life."

Was she kidding – this woman who always will be known as Tokyo Rose? No, the look on her face revealed that she wasn't.

CHAPTER XXXV

DeWOLFE'S DEATH

Tom DeWolfe died by his own hand in 1959. He was remembered for his role in the Tokyo Rose case. The story was below the center fold on page 43, column one.

"EX-U.S. AIDE A SUICIDE

T.E. DeWolfe, A Prosecutor

Helped Convict Tokyo Rose

"Seattle, June 19 (AP) – Tom E. DeWolfe, 56-year-old Government prosecutor who helped convict Tokyo Rose of treason after World War II, shot and killed himself in a downtown hotel room yesterday.

"In a note addressed to Coroner Leo M. Sowers, Mr. DeWolfe said he had been in ill health.

"Mr. DeWolfe retired in 1956 after working for the Justice Department for 29 years including six as a special assistant to the U.S. Attorney General. He was prosecutor in the treason trials of Robert H. Best and Douglas Chandler in connection with Radio Berlin broadcasts." [1]

EPILOGUE

On his last day as president, January 18, 1977, Gerald Ford pardoned Iva Toguri from her 27-year-old conviction as Tokyo Rose. Her citizenship was restored.

Wayne Collins did not live to see it. He died in 1974. But his son, Wayne Jr., took up the fight where his father left off, and at last, in the year of her greatest champion's death, Iva received solid backing from her own ethnic group.

The Japanese American Citizens League (30,000 strong) passed a resolution in 1974 to "Use its leadership, manpower, and resources to correct the miscarriage of justice in Iva Toguri's case".

The founder and leader of the JACL, Masao Satow, was swamped with other work – such as the repeal of Executive Order 9066. He fell ill in 1974, and died in March, 1976.

But a retired pediatrician from the state of Washington, Clifford Uyeda, took up the cause of a pardon for Iva Toguri, and with young Wayne Collins pressed it to a successful conclusion.

Dr. Uyeda formed the National Committee for Iva Toguri within the framework of the JACL. The committee financed and published a 32-page booklet, *Iva Toguri: Victim of a Legend*, then distributed it to every major newspaper in the U.S.

Conscientious newsmen everywhere in the country took a new interest in the case. The old news pattern of Iva, started by Clark Lee, which had prevailed over the facts for a third of a century, finally was reversed.

Editorials in support of her pardon were printed in the San Francisco *Chronicle*, Los Angeles *Times,* Honolulu *Advertiser,* the Denver *Post*, Wall Street *Journal*, the Seattle *Post-Intelligencer,* Chicago *Sun-Times*, the Washington *Star*, and many others.

The California legislature voted unanimously in favor of her pardon. U.S. Senators S.I. Hayakawa of California and Daniel Inouye of Hawaii, two-dozen congressmen, and virtually every high state official in California issued statements in support of the pardon.

Scores of organizations, including the Veterans of Foreign Wars (Willard Anderson Post #2471, Dalles, Oregon), the 41st Infantry Division Association, the VFW Nisei (Memorial Post #1629, Monterey Peninsula, Calif.) the VFW Nisei (Post #8985, Sacramento, Calif.), and the American Veterans Committee each issued proclamations in support of the pardon.

Uyeda credits the actual pardon to the timing and persistence of Wayne Collins, Jr.

"Wayne did not want to pressure President Ford into considering the pardon before the election," said Uyeda. "So, he waited until November 17th, 1976, then filed an official petition for the pardon to Lawrence M. Traylor, Pardon Attorney for the U.S. Justice Department, who sent it to U.S. Attorney General Edward H. Levi, who sent it to President Ford."

Its work done, the National Committee for Iva Toguri was dissolved. But Dr. Uyeda had a final thought about Iva after she had celebrated her pardon in San Francisco.

"In her loyalty to family, friends, and to her country," he reflected, "She is rather typical of the Nisei."

*   *   *

Having lived 36 years now in close touch with the legend of Tokyo Rose (28 of those 36 years with a thorough knowledge of Orphan Ann), it is the author's conviction that Iva Toguri will live to be honored by her fellow orphans of the World War II Pacific. The truth is out – and over the long haul, her simple faith has been justified. The truth has made her free, but in the case of Tokyo Rose, the truth needed a lot of help.

NOTES, PERIODICALS, BIBLIOGRAPHY

Chapter I

1. Honolulu Advertiser, Extra Edition, December 7, 1941
2. Fumi (or "Foumy") Saisho was a former University of Michigan student who became Radio Tokyo's principal female announcer and one of Shigetsugu Tsuneishi's interpreters. She went to work at Radio Tokyo in 1938 and broadcast as "Madame Tojo" throughout the war.
3. Roscoe, Theodore. U.S. Submarine Operations in World War II, Annapolis, Maryland, United States Naval Institute, 1949.
4. Ibid.
5. Klaas, Joseph, and Gervais, Joseph. Amelia Earhart Lives.
6. Morissey, Muriel (Amelia Earhart's sister). Courage Is The Price. George Palmer Putnam, Amelia's husband, made a three-day trek to reach a Marine Corps radio station near the coast of China, where broadcast reception from Radio,Tokyo was loud and clear. Mrs. Morissey wrote of Putnam's reaction, "After listening to the voice for less than a minute, GP said decisively, 'I'll stake my life that . . . is not Amelia's voice'."
7. Roscoe, Theodore, U.S. Submarine Operations in World War II, p. 71.
8. Ibid.
9. Yank Magazine, Pacific Edition, August 20, 1943
10. Lee, Clark, One Last Look Around, Duell, Sloan, and Pierce, New York, 1947, p. 90f.
11. The phrase, "Invincible Pearl Harbor", became a journalist's cliche in pre-war days. Predictions abounded that, if the Japanese should attack U.S. forces in the Pacific that, presumably, such an attack would have started in the Philippines, and the U.S. Navy would crush the Japanese navy within a matter of weeks.
12. The quotation was repeated commonly among men of the First U.S. Marine Division on Guadalcanal in August, 1942.
13. Another quotation which passed among First Division Marines at Cape Gloucester, New Britain, December 26, 1943.
14. Repeated among members of the 90th Bomb Group, Fifth U.S. Army Air Force during their move from Dobodura to Nadzab, New Guinea, January 17, 1944.
15. Commander Perry led a flight of Marine planes to their new base on Abemama, Gilbert Islands, December 29, 1943.
16. New York Times, March 27, 1944, bylined George F. Horne.

Chapter VI

1. From Zero Hour, Radio Tokyo, 02/22/44
2. From Zero Hour, Radio Tokyo, 03/09/44
3. From Zero Hour, Radio Tokyo, 03/10/44
4. From Zero Hour, Radio Tokyo, 03/14/44

5. From Zero Hour, Radio Tokyo, 03/18/44
6. From Zero Hour, Radio Tokyo, 05/22/44
7. From Zero Hour, Radio Tokyo, 03/24/44
8. From Zero Hour, Radio Tokyo, 03/25/44
9. From Zero Hour, Radio Tokyo, 03/27/44
10. From Zero Hour, Radio Tokyo, 03/30/44
11. From Zero Hour, Radio Tokyo, 04/10/44
12. From Zero Hour, Radio Tokyo, 04/21/44
13. From Zero Hour, Radio Tokyo, 05/12/44
14. Tsuneishi as witness for the prosecution, San Francisco, 07/07/49.
15. Cousens was gone from Zero Hour, and it showed.

Chapter VII

1. The contract between Harry Brundidge, Clark Lee, and Iva d'Aquino (witnessed by Phil d'Aquino and Leslie Nakashima), on September 1, 1945.
2. Iva Toguri to the author on January 2, 1959, at Chicago.
3. Los Angeles Examiner, September 3, 1945
4. Iva Toguri to the author or January 2, 1959, at Chicago. She was placed under custody of her husband for the night.

Chapter VIII

1. Myrtle Lipton was pictured on the cover of Yank Magazine, 06/29/45.
2. From the deposition for the defense of Iva Toguri by Kenneth Murayama, entered March, 1949, before Thomas W. Ainsworth, Vice Consul for the United States, Mitsui Main Bank Building, Room 335, Tokyo, in response to questions by Theodore Tamba for the defense.
3. From the deposition for the defense of Iva Toguri by George Kazumaro Uno, entered March 22, 1949, before Thomas W. Ainsworth, Mitsui Main Bank Building, Room 335, Tokyo, . . . questions by Tamba.

Chapter IX

1. Interview of Frederick Tilman in Tilman's home at Fowler, California, near Fresno in 1971. Tilman had retired from the FBI.
2. U.S. constitution, circa 1789, Article IV, Section I, Title 18.
3. The Treason Act of England, 1351
4. Charles Cousens faced lengthy hearings by an Australian military court, but was not charged for his broadcasting at Radio Tokyo. Wallace Ince was, threatened with a treason trial when he testified for the defense of Iva Toguri, but the threat was never carried out. Norman Reyes was not brought to trial in the Philippines and later became a resident of the United States.
5. Fumi Toguri had died en route to a relocation camp, shortly after being moved out of her Los Angeles home in the evacuations of March, 1942. Because she was in ill health and her death was listed as from natural

causes, it is a moot question how long she might have lived if she had been allowed to remain at home.

6. Martin Prey came to San Francisco to testify in Iva Toguri's defense, but was not allowed by the court to take the witness stand.
7. Department of Justice files, dated September 13, 1946.
8. From an Office Memorandum, Nathan T. Elliff, Chief, Internal Security Section, to Theron L. Caudie, Assistant Attorney General, Criminal Division, dated September 19, 1946.
9. From an Office Memorandum, Theron L. Caudie, Assistant Attorney General, to Attorney General Tom Clark, dated September 24, 1946.
10. From the Associated Press in Los Angeles, October 21, 1946.

Chapter X

1. From New Yorker Magazine, 1940, recalled at the time of Winchell's death at UCLA Medical Center on February 20, 1972. J. Edgar Hoover was a friend of Winchell's. However, virtually everybody in the public eye was either a friend or an enemy of the columnist. Winchell retired in 1969, and lived in seclusion in a Los Angeles hotel. His death resulted from prostrate cancer.
2. Winchell used the phrase "Soft on traitors" repeatedly in his broadcasts to describe a weak Justice Department under Attorney General Tom Clark.
3. From a memorandum by T. Vincent Quinn, assistant U.S. Attorney General, to the Secretary of State, dated October 24, 1947.
4. The article was released to all wire services and appeared in most major dailies in the United States, datelines Washington, December 3, 1947.
5. From a letter by James M. Carter, U.S. Attorney, Southern District of California, to Honorable Tom C. Clark, Attorney General, Department of Justice, dated December 5, 1947
6. From the Walter Winchell column in the Los Angeles Herald-Express, January 8, 1948.
7. From the Walter Winchell column in the Los Angeles Herald-Express, January 22, 1948.
8. From the Nashville Tennesseean, May 2, 1948.
9. The item was small, but it received widespread publication in U.S. daily newspapers.
10. This item also received widespread publication.

Chapter XI

1. From Brundidge's story of his meeting with Iva Toguri, the Nashville Tennesseean, May 5, 1948.
2. Ibid.
3. From the deposition for the defense of Iva Toguri by Tashikatsu Kodaira, entered March, 1949, before Thomas W. Ainsworth, Mitsui Main Bank Building, Room 335, Tokyo . . . questions by Tamba.
4. Ibid.

5. Letter from Earl Carroll to Iva Toguri, dated May 27, 1948. In June, on its approach to New York, a DC-6 with Earl Carroll aboard crashed into a transformer on a high power line at Mt. Carmel, Pennsylvania, killing Carroll and 42 others.

Chapter XII
1. From the <u>Nashville Tennessean</u>, May 2 and 5, 1949.
2. Iva Toguri to the author on January 3, 1959, at Chcago.
3. Iva Toguri to the author on January 3, 1959, at Chcago. Although she had known "Buddy" Uno in pre-war days in California, Iva did not trust him. She thought that he would only be using her to get back to the States. She had expressed   contempt for him ever since she saw him at Radio Tokyo dressed as a Japanese officer, with a sword dangling from his side, "like something from a Sabbatini novel", as Iva put it.
4. Iva's only child was stillborn in November, 1947.

Chapter XV
1. <u>San Francisco Chronicle</u>, September 26, 1948.
2. <u>Ibid.</u>
3. From Iva Toguri, Cell No. 3, San Francisco County Jail, October, 1948.
4. From a memo in the Department of Justice files, dated November 12, 1948, addressed simply to "Ray" and signed "Tom", in Tom DeWolfe's handwriting.
5. From an air mail letter, marked "Personal and Confidential", to Alexander M. Campbell, Esquire, Assistant Attorney General, Department of Justice, from Tom DeWolfe, dated November 12, 1948.

Chapter XVI
1. Late October, 1948. The prosecution released the story to all San Francisco papers.
2. Theodore Tamba to the author, October, 1949.
3. From the deposition for the defense of Iva Toguri by Lily Ghevenian, entered March   22, 1949, before Thomas W. Ainsworth, Mitsui Main Bank Building, Room 335, Tokyo . . . questions by Tamba.
4. From the deposition for the defense of Iva Toguri by Foumy Saisho, entered March 22, 1949, before Thomas W. Ainsworth, Mitsui Main Bank Building, Room 335, Tokyo . . . questions by Tamba.
5. Office memorandum, United States Government, from John B. Hogan to "The Files",   dated May 26, 1949.

Chapter XVII
1. Opening address of the Prosecution to the jury, United States . . . v. Iva Toguri, Treason, No. 31712-R.

Chapter XVIII
1. From the deposition for the defense, Katsuji Mori, vice chief of the Overseas Broadcast Planning Office at Radio Tokyo . . . questions by Tamba.

2. From the deposition for the defense, Tamotsu Murayama, former Associated Press newsman . . . questions by Tamba.
3. Tsuneishi's recollection of his speech to the Bunka Camp war prisoners, given in response to a question from Wayne Collins.
4. From the deposition for the defense, Nicholas Schenk, cook among the war prisoners at Bunka Camp . . . questions by Tamba.

Chapter XIX
1. Stanton Delaplane to the author at Delaplane's office in the Chronicle Building, San Francisco, December, 1958.
2. Lee, Clark. <u>One Last Look Around</u>, Duell, Sloan, and Pierce, New York, 1947, p. 90f.
3. Lee's interview notes on Iva, taken at the Imperial Hotel, September 1, 1945.
4. Lee, as evidenced in his book, knew that the name "Tokyo Rose" dated back to the earliest days of World War II in the Pacific.
5. What Lee knew about Brundidge's visit to Japan in March, 1948, would depend upon what he had heard from Brundidge and/or Hogan. Lee did not accompany them on that trip.
6. Stanton Delaplane to the author, December, 1958.

Chapter XX
1. From Overt Act No. 6 of the treason indictment against Iva Toguri, No. 31712-R.
2. As in this instance, Judge Michael Roche intervened several times on a patriotic theme during the testimony of a witness.
3. From Overt Act No. 6 of the treason indictment against Iva Toguri, No. 31712-R.

Chapter XXI
1. Recording of the "Zero Hour" broadcast, Radio Tokyo, August 11, 1944.
2. Recording of the "Zero Hour" broadcast, Radio Tokyo, August 16, 1944.
3. Recording of the "Zero Hour" broadcast, Radio Tokyo, August 15, 1944.

Chapter XXII
1. Phil Hanley, trial reporter for the <u>San Francisco News</u>.
2. The complete quote referred to nostalgic recollections of having ice cream sodas at "the corner drug store". Prosecution witness Ted E. Sherdeman testified that hurt his morale.
3. Marshall Hoot's recollection, testimony for the prosecution.
4. From Marshall Hoot's letter to his wife, dated December 29, 1943, from Abemama in the Gilbert Islands.
5. Quotation from Judge Michael J. Roche to Catherine Pinkham and the author at the Judge's office in the Federal Court Building, Seventh and Mission streets, San Francisco, December 22, 1958.

Chapter XXIII

1. Cousen's recollection from the witness stand, under questioning from Defense Counsel Wayne Collins.
2. Ibid.

Chapter XXV
1. From the trial transcript, Olshausen to Judge Roche, No. 31712-R
2. Phil Hanley's reporting of a conversation by phone with Harry Brundidge from the Monterey Country Club, California, September, 1949.

Chapter XXVI
1. Filipe (Phil) d'Aquino, witness for the defense, from the trial record, in response to questions by Wayne Collins.
2. Filipe (Phil) d'Aquino, witness for the defense, from the trial record, in response to questions by Wayne Collins.

Chapter XXVII
1. United Press, pre-trial interview by David Leonard with San Francisco County Jail matron Catherine Howerth.
2. Ibid.
3. Iva Toguri's recollection to the author, January 2-4, 1959.
4. From the description in the trial record by Charles Cousens.
5. From George K. Uno's deposition for the defense.
6. Iva Toguri's recollection from the witness stand.
7., 8., 9., 10. Ibid.

Chapter XXVIII
1. Clark Lee's notes, Exhibit 15, U.S. v. Iva Toguri, Treason, No. 31712R.
2. From the New York Times, October 24, 1944.
3. From the deposition for the defense, Toahikatsu Kodaira, March 22, 1949 . . questions by Tamba.
4. Roscoe, Theodore. U.S. Submarine Operations in World War II.
5. Orphan Ann script on the "Zero Hour", Radio Tokyo, February 22, 1944.
6. Navy "Citation" for Tokyo Rose of Radio Tokyo, released through Captain T. J. O'Brian, U.S.N., Director of Welfare, August 7, 1945.
7. Prosecution's summation to the jury, Frank J. Hennessy, Sept 22, 1949.

Chapter XXIX
1. From the instructions to the jury by the Honorable Michael J. Roche, Judge, Court Reporter's Transcript, Volume LIV, September 26-29, 1949.
2. Ibid.
3. Francis O'Gara to the author, December 22, 1958.
4. From Judge Roche's instructions to the jury.
5. John Mann to the author, December 23, 1958.
6. Iva Toguri to the author, January 2-4, 1959.
7. John Mann's note to Judge Roche, 2nd day of Deliberations, Oct 4, 1949.
8. John Mann's recollection to the author, December 23, 1958.
9. Judge Roche to the jury, second evening of deliberations, October 4, 1949.

10. Ibid.
11. John Mannis note to Judge Roche on the third day of deliberation
12. Instructions to the jury by the Honorable Michael J. Roche, Judge, Court
    Reporter's Transcript, Volume LIV, September 26-29, 1949.
13. Ibid.
14. Judge Roche to the jury on the third day of deliberations, October 5, 1949.
15. From John Mann's request for additional instructions to Judge Roche.
16. Judge Roche to the jury, third evening of deliberations, October 5, 1949.
17. John Mann to the author, December 23, 1958.
18. San Francisco Chronicle, October 6, 1949.
19.Catherine Pinkham to the author, December 22, 1958.
20. Paine Knickerbocker to the author, December 22, 1958.
21. Bill Bancroft to the author, December 23, 1958.
22. San Francisco Chronicle, October 6, 1949.
23. Paul Brook of the San Francisco Examiner, October 6, 1949.
24. Iva Toguri to Bailiff Herbert Cole and Cole's wife en route to Alderson,
    West Virginia.
25. Herbert Cole to the author, Sir Frances Drake Hotel, San Franciso,
    December 23, 1958.
26. Ibid.

Chapter XXX
1., 2., 3., 4., 5.   Iva Toguri to the author, Chicago, January 2-4, 1959.
6. Iva Toguri in a San Franciso press conference at the home of Wayne Collins,
    January, 1956.

Chapter XXXI
1. John Mann in a letter to U.S. Attorney General Herbert Brownell, March 7,
    1956.
2. Invitation to Iva Toguri from Co-chairman Don Cunningham and Paul Yale,
    41st National Guard, Oregon, to their annual reunion on June 17, 1956.
3. Resolution by the Springfield, Ohio, American Legion Post, February, 1956.
4. Katherine Pinkham to the author

Chapter XXXII
1. John Mann to the author, San Francisco, December 23, 1958.
2. From John Mann's letter sent to relatives following the trial, 1949.
3. John Mann to Catherin Pinkham.
4. From John Mann's letter sent to relatives following the trial, 1949

Chapter XXXIV
1. Seattle Post-Intelligencer, June 20, 1959.

ABOUT THE COVER

Following the Japanese attack on Pearl Harbor, American submariners in the China Seas had visions of an enemy siren who broadcasted her taunts to American sailors by radio from Japan. That was the beginning of the legend of **Tokyo Rose**. In the years that followed, similar visions were shared by millions of fighting men in the Pacific. They spread the fame of **Tokyo Rose** to the entire allied world.

Artist Larry Winkler's version of the legendary **Tokyo Rose** (reproduced on the front cover), spans 2,800 years in its merger of the Pacific war siren with the classical Greek vision of a siren's attack on Ulysses and his fellow voyagers . . . trying to get past the siren's call.

Homer wrote the lines for that scene 2,800 years before World War II in *The Odyssey*, circa 900 B.C., Book III.

> "Our prime duty will be to turn a deaf ear
>   to their singing
> Only myself may listen, after you have so
>   fastened me
> With tight-drawn cords that I stand
>   immovably secured to the mast,
> And if I beg you or bid you let me loose,
> Then you must redoubly firm me into place,
>   with yet more bonds.
> I repeated this till all had heard it well,
> While our trim ship was borne toward
>   the island of those Siren-sisters ...."

Pictured on the back cover stands the woman cast by her own country as a traitorous **Tokyo Rose**. She is Iva Ikuko Toguri, American born on the fourth of July, 1916. In this photo she stands outside of Sugamo Prison in Tokyo in 1946, when it was thought that all her troubles with the U.S. Government were over.

There is no greater irony in history than the treason trial of Iva Toguri. Although she was a civilian when she was trapped in wartime Japan, in her dogged loyalty to her country she was typical of the American Nisei who served the United States during World War II.

www.ingramcontent.com/pod-product-compliance
Lightning Source LLC
LaVergne TN
LVHW051520080426
835509LV00017B/2130